WHISPERS FROM
Heaven
Stories to Lift Your Spirit

PUBLICATIONS INTERNATIONAL, LTD.

Picture credits:

Front cover: **Christian Michaels/FPG International** (inset).

Ann Barrow: 69; **Eddie Corkery:** 65, 103, 143, 155, 175, 190, 198, 212, 218, 227, 247; **Todd Leonardo:** 90; **Margery Mintz:** Table of contents, 158; **Jan Stamm:** Table of contents, 8, 13, 20, 25, 31, 33, 39, 43, 47, 49, 55, 83, 86, 94, 101, 105, 110, 115, 119, 135, 139, 149, 152, 167, 179, 186, 195, 204, 216, 233, 239, 245, 250, 261, 264, 271, 282; **SuperStock:** Leslie Braddock: 17; John Bunker: 171; Camera di Commercio, Milan/Fratelli Alinari: 129; Christie's Images: 253; **Linda Warner:** 78, 285; **Jody Wheeler:** Table of contents, 58, 75, 125, 163, 257, 279.

Louis Weber, C.E.O.
Publications International, Ltd.
7373 North Cicero Avenue
Lincolnwood, Illinois 60712

Permission is never granted for commercial purposes.

Manufactured in China.

8 7 6 5 4 3 2 1

ISBN: 0-7853-3994-9

Library of Congress Catalog Card Number: 99-75915

CONTENTS

◇ ◇ ◇

A QUIET PROMISE

◈ ◈ ◈

*T*HERE IS, as any wilderness explorer knows, an easy way and a hard way to travel. You can do it alone or together; relying only on what you know, or accepting help and guidance from a companion. Wilderness explorers hire guides; life explorers seek God. *Whispers from Heaven: Stories to Lift Your Spirit* will inspire you along your journey, through stories shared by those who have had their lives changed, spirits lifted, and hope fulfilled.

During life's journey, we are guided by faith as we learn to listen and watch for signs of hope. All we have to do is trust in God's promises, knowing he has a plan for each of our lives and will send us companions when we need them. Upheld by angels all around, we realize that hope has a face and healing has hands. We learn that troubles can be redeemed into useful, positive lessons of life to support our growth and wisdom.

Turning the pages of *Whispers from Heaven*, you will be awed by examples of the gift of love—to heal, guide, comfort, and teach, to transform and renew lives. You will also read about those brave travelers whose triumphant journey of recovery shows that illnesses or accidents are part of the varied landscape of our lives.

So pause quietly for a moment and know that God is nearby. These whispers from heaven are as close as a prayerful thought, a friend's hand, a loved one's presence. Whether in the heights of prosperity or the depths of despair, God's quiet promise endures: "I am with you always."

◈ ◈ ◈ ◈

"I am with you always, even to the end of the age."
—Matthew 28:20

◈ ◈ ◈ ◈

GUIDED BY FAITH

◆ ◆ ◆

I BELIEVE IN GOD *as I believe in my friends because I feel the breath of his affection, feel his invisible and intangible hand, drawing, leading me, grasping me, because I possess an inner conscious-ness of a particular providence and of a universal mind that marks out for me the course of my destiny.*

—MIGUEL DE UNAMUNO

THE TALE OF THREE TREES
An American Folktale

◆   ◆   ◆

THREE LITTLE TREES stood high upon a mountain discussing their dreams for the future. The first little tree looked up at the dazzling night sky and said, "I want to carry the treasure of kings and queens. I want to be beautiful. I want to be filled with all the riches in the world."

The nearby stream caught the second little tree's eye. "I want to be a mighty sailing vessel," he said. "I want to sail in the roaring oceans, roam the high seas, and deliver kings and queens safely to their destinations."

The third little tree loved the mountaintop. "I want to stay right here and grow and grow and grow," she said. "I want the people that pass by to look at me touching heaven and think of God."

One day, many years later, three powerful lumberjacks came to help the three trees with the next season of their lives.

The first tree, now stunningly beautiful, was cut down. "I will become the most beautiful treasure chest," he thought. "I will get to hold all the world's riches."

The mighty second tree was cut down. "I will now sail the roaring oceans," thought the tree. "I will be the mightiest of all sailing vessels."

The third tree, with her branches stretched toward heaven, was also cut down. Together with the other two trees, she was taken down the lovely hillside.

The first tree arrived at a carpenter's shop. The beautiful tree was aglow with excitement. But he wasn't made into a treasure chest. The skillful carpenter made the beautiful tree into an ordinary feeding trough.

The second tree was brought to a shipyard. The mighty second tree thought, "Now, I will be the most vigorous of vessels." But the strong second tree was made into a simple fishing boat.

The third tree was brought to a lumberyard. There she was made into beams and put aside. "Why did this happen?" thought the third tree. "All I ever wanted was to touch heaven."

As the weeks passed, their dreams began to fade from memory. However, one magical night brought the first tree's dream to life. A young mother put her newborn into the trough. "This manger is perfect," said the mother to her husband. And the first tree *knew* he was cradling the most important treasure ever.

One night the fishing boat was used by a tired traveler and his friends. They quickly fell asleep, and the small boat floated out to sea. The sea became rough, and a thunderstorm was brewing. This frightened the second tree. If only he were a mighty vessel and could withstand the force of the storm! The traveler was awakened by the storm, and he stretched out his arms and said, "Peace." The sea became calm, and the thunderstorm vanished. It was then that the second tree realized he was carrying the Almighty King.

On a Friday morning, the third tree was taken by soldiers and carried through a hostile mob. She trembled with fear and distaste as a man's hands were nailed to her. But the following Sunday the sun rose. The Earth was full of joy. She realized that everything had changed because of God's love.

The first tree was made beautiful.

The second tree was made mighty.

The third tree made people think of God.

THE RIVER OF KINDNESS:
Terri Hout's Life of Gentle Ministry

◇　◇　◇

RIGHTENED, hurting, hopeless. That's how Terri Hout felt as a young woman who turned to drugs and alcohol in order to deaden the pain of abusive relationships and the loss of a dream. But then strong arms encircled her and turned her gently around. Today, Terri is a mature and radically changed woman who, in her job as an area director for Prison Fellowship Ministries, helps others whose lives are as bleak as hers once was.

She says, "It's a privilege to be able to make a difference in other peoples' lives. I made so many mistakes, so many wrong decisions for which there were consequences that I live with every day. And yet there is the joy of God's grace and mercy being used in the lives of others. You can allow your past to hold you prisoner or you can give it to the Lord and let him make something beautiful and useful from it."

Prison Fellowship is a nondenominational agency that was founded by Watergate conspirator Chuck Colson after he spent time in prison for white-collar crimes he committed as an aide to President Nixon. Behind bars, Colson has said, he saw firsthand how desperately his fellow prisoners needed a relationship with Christ and also needed the practical skills that lead to productive lives.

Today, Terri helps Colson bring those twin missions about by directing Prison Fellowship in Iowa and South Dakota. She does everything

◇　◇　◇　◇

"I was afraid that if I became a Christian, I'd botch it up like I'd botched up everything else."

◇　◇　◇　◇

from recruitment and training of volunteers to fund-raising to hands-on work with inmates—playing her guitar and singing and leading seminars on such topics as developing a work ethic, parenting from the inside, and planning a new life on the outside.

It was a long and winding road, however, that brought Terri to this point. In fact, at the same time the Watergate scandal was teaching Colson some hard lessons, Terri was battling demons of her own. Terri, whose adolescence was tumultuous due to a difficult relationship with her step-father, began to use alcohol as a teenager. She escaped into military service after graduation to fulfill her dream of a career in medicine.

Stationed in Okinawa as an operating room technician, Terri helped treat terrified young soldiers who had been wounded in battle in Vietnam. Although she was using drugs and alcohol off duty, Terri was still in control at work. She had a genuine gift for healing and helping others. Instinctively able to say and do the right thing in a medical emergency, Terri dreamed of a career in health care back home in Iowa when her military service was over. But problems that had developed with her knees became more serious when she returned to the United States. When Terri could no longer stand for hours at a time, her doctor ordered her to stop doing hospital work and find a desk job.

By the time she began training for her job as an accounting clerk with an insurance company, Terri—then in her mid-twenties—was in rough shape. She was estranged from her family, depressed, often ill, involved with one toxic boyfriend after another, and using alcohol and drugs. She could barely hold herself together at her new job. "Wrong living" is the way she sums it up.

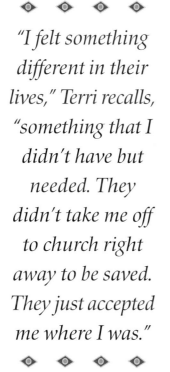

"I felt something different in their lives," Terri recalls, "something that I didn't have but needed. They didn't take me off to church right away to be saved. They just accepted me where I was."

The coworker who trained her, Marilyn Runyan, was a single woman in her forties who lived with two career-women friends. She could see how troubled Terri was. She also saw something else. "She was a bit of a loner—every day she went home for lunch. And I knew she had some health problems. Yet her potential—her alertness and willingness to learn—were very evident from the beginning."

Marilyn and her friends soon began to make some quiet, simple gestures that caught Terri's attention—and her heart. "She lived in a drafty apartment and often she came down with bad colds. We would take her hot soup, sometimes bring her home with us if she was sick, and just generally make sure she was getting along all right," Marilyn recalls. As Terri became more comfortable around them, she played her guitar and sang for them, and they encouraged her budding musical talent.

"I felt something different in their lives," Terri recalls, "something that I didn't have but needed. They didn't take me off to church right away to be saved. They just accepted me where I was." When Terri asked, the three friends told her about their beliefs, but they never pushed.

Christmas approached, and one night Terri was sitting alone at her kitchen table with a bottle of vodka and a supply of illegally obtained prescription drugs. "I was afraid that if I became a Christian, I'd botch it up like I'd botched up everything else. Still, I couldn't forget what I'd witnessed. I prayed for Jesus to come into my heart, and then I found myself standing on their doorstep with a Bible. They told me where to start reading and invited me to their church."

"There was no flash of lightning," as Marilyn remembers it. "We just gave her a cup of cold water and she drank."

Before long, Terri was singing at her friends' church and at nursing homes. By the 1980s her confidence had grown to the point where she was able to make two albums of Christian music. It was her love of music that brought her to her present job. "After I heard about Prison Fellowship on the radio, I called its office and asked if they ever needed music at their seminars."

They did. When Terri discovered she had a heart for this sort of work, her volunteerism evolved into the full-time job she holds today. Now in her forties, she helps younger women just as Marilyn and her friends—who are still like surrogate mothers to Terri—once helped her.

One example is Jenny, a young woman who came to a life-planning seminar Terri conducted at a women's reformatory. Jenny, who was involved with an abusive boyfriend at the time she committed her crime, was imprisoned for aiding and abetting in an armed robbery at the age of 19. Just as the young Terri had done, Jenny dreamed of making a career in medicine, but she feared that her felony conviction would prevent her from ever being licensed as a nurse.

With Terri's help, Jenny set up hearings with the state licensing board, attended nursing school at night while working as an aide in nursing homes, and finally graduated last spring. "It was so hard, after my release, to go before the nursing board to tell my story, but Terri told me that she would keep me in her thoughts and prayers so that she knew I

"It's been such a thrilling experience to watch Terri grow," Marilyn says, "because she did a real 180-degree turn. We are so proud of her and her accomplishments."

could be strong. From the beginning, Terri told me that when I graduated she would be in the front row cheering. And she was. She was sitting right beside my mom—they've become very close. I think of her as a second mother."

These days, Jenny—who is now 27—continues the cycle of helping by offering reassurance to the patients in her care on a medical-surgical floor. Sometimes just a comforting smile and the squeeze of her hand gives them some of the strength that Terri had given to her. "I just love my job!" Jenny exclaims. "I deal with people who are scared because they are going into surgery. I just let them know that I'm there before they go in, and that I'll be there when they come back out. Sometimes they just need to know that somebody who cares is there."

Over the years, Terri's relationships with her own family members have healed and strengthened; she and her mother are close today. Terri and her three guardian angels, who are now all retired, have also remained as close as family. And when she's in town, Terri drops by to see them almost every day. "It's been such a thrilling experience to watch Terri grow," Marilyn says, "because she did a real 180-degree turn. We are so proud of her and her accomplishments."

All of this hope and healing came about because Marilyn and her friends gave Terri's parched soul a cup of cold water. When she drank, the cup didn't empty but filled back up so that she could offer it to the next weary traveler to come along. There will always be those who thirst. And there will always be those like Marilyn, Terri, and Jenny, who make sure that the river of kindness never runs dry.

BY REBECCA CHRISTIAN

NEVER WALK ALONE

◆ ◆ ◆

BARBARA ALWAYS BELIEVED she was a good Christian. She was raised as such, and she had reached the point where she honestly thought she had her spiritual life in order. She believed in God, went to church, and tried to do the right thing—she seemed to be an all-around religiously correct person.

Barbara raised her children the same way she'd been raised. They went to church and attended Bible school. Barbara had the perfect Christian family. Or did she?

Barbara's husband was not interested in church or religion or belief in a "higher power." As time went on, he became less "neutral" about his beliefs and actually started to speak out against the idea of Christianity.

The reality of Barbara's belief system began to be strained. She knew that she was following some enlightened path, but she began to have doubts as to what it actually was. Attending church alone began to wear her down emotionally. Each week, she would muster up the energy to prepare the children for Sunday services, only to be met by moans and groans of, "Why do we have to go if Daddy doesn't?"

It became an ongoing battle, and by the time she finally dropped the children off at Sunday school, Barbara was more drained than ever. Each week, it took more and more effort to become part of the congregation. What made it even more difficult was that they lived in a small community, and the absence of her spouse was obvious.

People arrived at church *together*, Barbara observed, unless, of course, they had no spouse. It probably was not as evenly divided as it seemed, but at that point it appeared to her that everyone else was happy, joyous, and showing up at church together with love in their hearts.

That was something Barbara wanted more than anything. She wanted to arrive at church with her husband by her side, and share the weekly religious experience with him. But the chance of this taking place was next to none, and Barbara knew it.

She continued to participate in the activities of her church and took on a full religious schedule. She taught classes for the second graders, headed up a community action group for her block, served on the church council, and did Bible readings once a month from the pulpit.

So what was missing? Why did Barbara always feel a void? There was a void because her husband did not share her enthusiasm. There was a void because she was always rushing around and getting nowhere. There was a void because as much as she *believed* and *attended* and *did*—something spiritual was missing. However, she did not understand that yet.

She did not know the difference between religion and spirituality. She did not even know there was a difference. Barbara was becoming miserable, and she had no idea why.

She talked about God. She talked about believing. She talked about praying. But she did not really know how to pray, or believe, or walk with God. She assumed that if she just continued to do what she had always done, God would make things the way she wanted them to be.

Barbara's idea of praying was to bargain: "If I do this, God, will you do that?" Unfortunately, she did not realize that God does not make deals. In fact, he says as much in the Lord's Prayer: "Thy kingdom come, Thy will be done." Thy will be done? Whose will?

Not Barbara's will. She did not understand this, however, until one Sunday when the true power of spirituality was revealed to her.

She took her children to Sunday school as usual. She sat in church as usual. Yet, on this particular day, no one chose to sit near her. The usual perfect-looking couples were everywhere. Barbara felt deserted and miserable and alone.

She began praying with her typical, "Dear God, please make me happy, send my husband to church, make my children do well in school," etc. Barbara spent a lot of time telling God what to do. She never realized that God likes to be in charge of the plans he's laid out.

In Barbara's church, the Lord's Prayer is a meaningful, community-connected prayer. Everyone holds hands and recites the prayer together as one. Unfortunately for Barbara on this particular day, there was no one sitting next to her on either side. There was no one even close enough in front of her or behind her to reach across the benches and grab ahold of. This was an unusual morning, and Barbara was feeling particularly sad and alone.

As the congregation recited the prayer, holding hands, Barbara simply stretched out her arms, palms up, and joined in the recitation. As she prayed, a strange sensation took hold of her. She felt one of her hands being grasped. She felt a tiny jolt running through her body, and the hair on her arms began to tingle. She found herself lost in the prayer.

The Spirit truly acknowledged her and she, in turn, realized what it meant when she said, "Thy will be done."

At the completion, she looked around, searchingly, for the person who had moved next to her to grasp her hand. No one was there; no one was on either side of her. No one had moved to the front or back of her. She still stood alone, but she was not alone. Someone had held her hand. Someone was there to keep her company. Someone was showing her the difference between going through the motions and having the inner peace of knowing what it is like to have the Spirit with her.

Barbara was fraught with emotion; she did not know what to do next. But she didn't have to do anything. She was filled with peace. She was overjoyed. She knew she had been filled with something she could never provide on her own. The Spirit truly acknowledged her and she, in turn, realized what it meant when she said, "Thy will be done."

That day, Barbara learned that she does not have to have someone physically sitting next to her. Her husband does not have to attend church with her, and her children do not have to be perfect academic specimens. That's not what is important. She still works diligently for the church and its many projects her basic routine hasn't changed much. However, Barbara knows it is not her will that is giving her direction. She has learned that God is with her all the time, and it is his will being done.

On that Sunday, she finally understood the difference between religion and spirituality. God truly was with her, and he gave her inner peace. She will never walk alone again.

BY ELIZABETH TOOLE

AN ANSWER TO A STRANGER'S PRAYER

◇ ◇ ◇

EVA RESTLESSLY PACED back and forth across her living room floor. She couldn't get to sleep. Her family was besieged with health and financial problems, and there seemed to be no solutions in sight. Eva was a churchgoing woman, but lately it seemed as though her prayers were just empty, powerless words. Could God hear her cries of pain? Did he care? Was God even real?

Eva's faith had never been so low in all of her 50-some years of life. Her thoughts turned to Larry, her missing ex-husband. Neither she nor her family had heard from him in over ten years. Was he still alive, she wondered, or had the alcohol finally killed him like it had killed their marriage? Eva had never remarried, and her love for Larry had gradually faded to familial concern—after all, he was the father of her only child, Larry Jr.

Larry Jr. was a father himself now, with a precious little boy who had never seen his grandfather. Eva sighed. Maybe it was for the better, but still...she couldn't help but wonder what had happened to her ex-husband. She chided herself for her lack of faith. God was the only hope she had. Finally, she laid back on the couch in her Anderson, South Carolina, home and stared up at the ceiling.

"Dear Lord," she prayed, "please let our family know if Larry is alive or not." She knew her only son needed to know if his father was still alive.

At one time her son was planning to go into the ministry, and he'd even attended a Christian college for a few years, but he eventually fell away from God. The problems their family suffered only seemed to cement Larry Jr.'s belief that God was remote and uncaring. Now only God and a mother's prayers could provide the answers the family needed.

Little did Eva know that God was already arranging an answer to her prayer, hundreds of miles away.

That same evening, my husband, Kevin, and I were walking down the streets of the historic French Quarter in New Orleans, enjoying a much-needed vacation. The sun was rapidly fading behind the clouds, and we quickened our steps to reach the hotel before dark. The streets that had seemed quite safe in the daylight were now becoming bedrooms for the homeless.

As Kevin discussed his plans to lead a group of teenagers on a missionary trip to Quito, Ecuador, the following summer, I began to feel God tugging at my heart. The more my husband talked about the evangelistic crusade, the heavier my heart felt. I suddenly stopped on the sidewalk and turned toward my husband.

"Kevin, I feel so guilty. Here we're talking about witnessing to the people in South America, but look at all these homeless people we're walking by that also need to know about God's love."

Kevin looked around him and then looked back at me. It was as if he had been so engrossed in his conversation that he hadn't even seen the people bedding down in the street. They were such a common sight in

> *"Dear Lord," she prayed, "please let our family know if Larry is alive or not."*

the French Quarter that after a while they became almost invisible. As tourists, we'd been cautioned to walk quickly past the homeless and to stay off the streets after dark. We had heard horror stories of muggings—and worse—that others had suffered who hadn't heeded this rule. But that night there was a divine plan in motion that not even fear could stop.

"You're right," Kevin soberly agreed. "Let's stop and talk to the next homeless person we see."

With hearts pounding, the two of us walked forward in the fading light. Ahead, a man wearing ragged clothes sat on a trash can outside a bar. As we drew closer, we heard the man calling out for money. Most people walked quickly past him, looking away, but when he spoke to us, we smiled at him encouragingly.

We soon discovered that the man was drunk and very talkative. We asked general questions about him and his life, but waited to reveal that we were Christians. I silently prayed for God to give us the opening we needed to witness to him.

Suddenly, I couldn't believe my ears. The hairs on my arm stood straight up as I heard the man, whose name was Larry, tell me about his son, Larry Jr., who had attended a Christian college in Tennessee.

"Why, my husband and I both went to that college!" I exclaimed. "When did your son attend?"

Larry scratched his unshaven chin and thought for a minute. "It was in the early '80s."

Again I was dumbfounded. "That's when we attended," I said. "What is your son's name?"

Larry replied, "Larry Grimm, Jr."

The name rang a bell in our memories. What were the odds of this happening? There were less than 1,000 students who had attended the college during that time. We both knew it had to be God who had divinely orchestrated this moment.

The longer we talked, the more sober Larry became. We bought him dinner and talked with him about the Lord. We learned that he had been living on the street and he hadn't talked to his family in over ten years.

When we returned to our Florida home a few days later, I contacted the college's alumni association for Larry Jr.'s last known address. Then I called the Anderson, South Carolina, number that the college had provided. After a few rings, a woman answered.

"You don't know me," I began excitedly, "but I'm calling to tell you that last Thursday night we met a man who I believe is your ex-husband."

The woman on the other end of the line began to sob.

After I told her about the encounter with her husband, Eva told me how, on that same evening, she had prayed for God to let her know if Larry was still alive.

"Now I know that God really does hear and answer my prayers," she exclaimed. "My son will know where his father is and that he is alive."

Eva explained the difficulties her family had endured and how they had begun to wonder if God really cared. We prayed together over the phone, and she told me that this experience would give her the strength to keep going and to trust in God again. I realized then how important it is to respond to those tuggings in my heart, since I never know who or what I might find at the other end of the heartstrings.

BY REGINA M. BALLARD

"Now I know that God really does hear and answer my prayers," she exclaimed. "My son will know where his father is and that he is alive."

TRANSPLANTED

❖ ❖ ❖

*I*N JULY 1971, I was offered a second chance for life two times—first with the gift of a kidney transplant, and then with the gift of eternal salvation. I didn't receive either gift very well.

At the time, I was a graduate student at the University of Washington, awaiting a kidney transplant. While hooked up to a kidney machine, I had been summoned into Seattle's University Hospital nine times in two years for a possible transplant. After nine "scrubbed missions," I was hardly enthused when I received my tenth call. But on Wednesday, July 8, 1971, we finally went through with the operation.

The hospital admitted me as fast as I could scribble my signature. After being in surgery for seven-and-a-half hours, I awakened in my hospital room with my new kidney.

But it didn't function.

The physicians assured me this was not necessarily a bad omen. The kidney could be under some trauma and would probably recover shortly.

As I sat on my bed pondering my prospects, a man in a suit sauntered in. He stood at the side of my bed, smiling at me pleasantly. *Who is this guy?* I thought.

"Hello, Gary," the man said gently. He opened a conspicuous Bible. "They call me Chaplain." I grimaced. He must have noticed because he hesitated, but he kept on smiling.

"I'm sorry," I said, "but I'm not interested in your religion. Have a good day, though."

Without argument, the man handed me his card and walked out of my room, still smiling. I shook my head sadly as I watched him depart. *What some people do for a living*, I thought.

Despite the physicians' optimism, setbacks soon hit me hard. The blood flow in one of my tubes declined, and I began to bleed externally. My potassium level soared, and I could not raise my feet and legs from my bed. My blood pressure fluctuated, leaving me light-headed when standing, and with head pain—despite an array of ice packs—when I was lying on my bed. My main anti-rejection medicine, prednisolone, made my thinking muddled and cloudy.

Each problem was surpassed by another just as bad. The anti-rejection shots in my hip left me sore, screaming, and sullen. My daily liquid restriction (just 450cc) barely wet my parched throat. The persistent sunshine beaming into the room made me sweat, and my fan sent hot, stuffy air into my lungs. The noise from the new construction outside increasingly annoyed me as the days wore on.

"I'm sorry," I said, "but I'm not interested in your religion. Have a good day, though."

Surprisingly, my kidney did not reject my body, even though it did not function. It was almost as though it was waiting for something. *But waiting for what?* I wondered.

As I continued to deteriorate physically, what little enthusiasm I had evaporated. Ignored by me and wary of my cynicism and depression, my friends soon stopped visiting. Even my nurses seemed elusive.

But I'd make it without them, I told myself. No amount of suffering would handcuff me. I'd pull through. I always had.

One evening after I'd survived a particularly tough day, my rock radio station played the song "The Old Rugged Cross." The deejay was trying to be funny, but I wasn't in the mood for his brand of humor. The song's words irritated me, and I shut off the radio in disgust. But for a moment I wondered…what if there really was something to God?

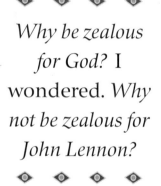

Why be zealous for God? I wondered. Why not be zealous for John Lennon?

Later, images of my boyhood experience in church began flashing through my mind. I envisioned the pastor praying behind the pulpit and some farmers sleeping in the pews. I saw myself reciting scriptures for Sunday school. I hadn't thought about "church stuff" in years. Why now?

On July 30, at about 10:30 at night, I happened to glance into my full-length mirror. A shriveled form with a bewildered, vacant stare looked back. I pressed my fingers on my cheek apprehensively.

"God, why have you forsaken me?" I moaned. For emphasis, I gestured with my bony right hand.

Then I wandered to the window. Without too much effort, I thought, a fit person could climb onto the window seat, slip through the open lower window, push out the screen, and dive onto the pavement two stories below. I sat on the window seat and let my tears escape. For some reason I recalled a service at the church I'd attended as a grade-schooler. I remembered the pastor fervently reading aloud from an oversized black Bible. I never knew who he was talking to or what he was talking about, because I never paid attention. Religion was for grown-ups. But why was it for anyone at all? *Why be zealous for God?* I wondered. *Why not be zealous for John Lennon?*

I tried to stop thinking, but I really didn't want to stop. These thoughts helped me forget my current troubles. What if there really *was* something to religion? I couldn't push that thought out of my mind.

As I slid across the window seat, I cringed in pain. Biting my lip, I struggled to stand, and I turned toward the lower window. I grabbed the top of the window frame and attempted to lift one of my legs up to the window seat. Quickly exhausted, I slumped hard to the floor. After a while, I climbed back on the window seat. Yet, even by pulling with both hands, I could not lift my leg.

There was no way I could reach the lower window. There was no way I could help myself.

I slid off the window seat and fell to the floor. In a whisper I cried, "God, help me! I'll do anything! Please!" As I crawled back into bed, everything was quiet. An unfamiliar peace began spreading gently within me.

The next morning, the sunshine was skipping on the wall and all the nurses and doctors seemed more cheerful. I was puzzled by their suddenly upbeat attitudes. Then I realized the Lord was already answering my prayer of the previous night, and it was my outlook that was improving.

Sitting on my bed the following day, I had a strange urge. I needed the urinal! Frantically, I rustled through the drawers of my bedside cabinet until I located it. Almost awestruck, I carefully used it. Then I sat open-mouthed and stared across the room. Suddenly I realized that I needed to tell a nurse. I leaped from my bed and promptly collapsed to the floor. But stretching out on my side and pushing with my hands, I eventually reached the door. I waved the small, plastic urinal in the hallway.

"I did it!" I yelled. A nurse ran to see what the commotion was, and removed the tilted pitcher from my hand. She rejoiced with me. "You did it!" A doctor came from an adjoining room. "I did it!" I said, pointing proudly to the urinal in the nurse's hand. The doctor grinned. "Yes, you certainly did!"

Since my transplanted kidney began functioning that first week in August 1971, I have never experienced a rejection symptom. The kidney I received belonged to a motorcyclist who died in an accident and was a "D" match, the worst match ever given to a transplant patient at that time.

Over the years, as I've gotten to know the Lord better, I've come to believe that there were two things within me in that hospital room: a kidney that was in place and not working, and the relationship with God that I had buried inside me since my youth. I tried to reject both, but neither rejected me. Now the continual functioning of my kidney is a sign to me of God's faithfulness, mercy, and enduring love. Though medication and aging may take their toll on my body, my kidney works on, and my soul is healthy and thriving. How thankful I am that I was given a new chance for life, both on this earth and forever in heaven.

BY GARY SEVERSON

LISTENING TO THAT STILL, SMALL VOICE

❖ ❖ ❖

IT WAS LATE SATURDAY afternoon when the pleasant-looking young lady with long chestnut hair caught my attention—or rather the ankle-to-knee purple wrap over her leg cast caught it. She was hobbling slowly on her crutches down the sloping sidewalk leading to the post office.

I flashed a smile toward her as I reached for my car door. "That looks like a real pain," I called to her.

"You're right, it is," she chuckled. Then, reaching the bench in front of my car, she called back, "You wouldn't happen to have change for a ten-dollar bill, would you? I need to buy postage stamps from the machine."

"No, sorry. I only have a twenty," I replied as I closed the door and put my key in the ignition.

"Oh well, I'll just sit here until someone comes along."

Stop. Elaine, you dummy. What's keeping you from running across the street to get change for her? The message came from out of the blue, tugging at my conscience.

She was shocked to see me reopen the car door and walk toward her. "I'll be happy to run and get change for you from the grocery store."

"Oh, you don't have to do that. Someone will probably come with change pretty soon," she replied.

❖ ❖ ❖ ❖

I knew that, whether it was instinct or the Spirit guiding me, I was right to follow it.

❖ ❖ ❖ ❖

"I'd like to, really. . . . It'll just take a minute. Wait—let me check the machine first."

It took only three quick steps for me to reach the post office door and see the big "Out of Order" sign taped to the stamp dispenser. "Sorry, but there are no stamps here. The machine is out of order again."

In the next couple minutes we brainstormed other possibilities. But on our little Northwest island, there appeared to be no other place to buy stamps.

Wait, Elaine. What's wrong with looking in your purse and giving her yours? There it was again—the still, small voice.

The young woman continued talking to me. "That figures. I've had nothing but bad luck since I moved here. I nearly froze to death in the winter storm. My landlord was in California and I had no water or electricity. Then I had this accident and now I can't even drive to get around for another 45 days. People here are so unfriendly. I'd be better off moving to another state."

I breathed a quick prayer for just the right words to respond to her. "Just a minute," I broke in. "I have some stamps in my purse in the car. Let me get them so you can mail the letters that you need to today."

"I have a little bit of change. I can buy one from you. Oh, and here's my lucky silver dollar. You can take that, too," she said.

"No. I don't need your money. Here—take three or four extra," I insisted as I tore several stamps from the little booklet I had retrieved from my car.

Give her your business card. There it was again—the still, small voice. I was getting more involved than I had meant to. But, listening to the prod-

Sitting down on the bench beside her, my schedule no longer seemed to matter as much as this lonely new neighbor.

dings of that inner voice, I handed the woman the card with my phone number on it.

She looked it over. "Christian Writers Consultant," it said under my name. "Oh! No wonder—you're a Christian. The only other person to be nice to me this week was a Christian, too—Reverend Baker, the pastor at the Baptist church."

Sitting down on the bench beside her, my schedule no longer seemed to matter as much as this lonely new neighbor. I was genuinely interested in the concerns of this woman, her background, and her travels around the world. I discovered that Denise was interested in animals and had become a volunteer at the Humane Society to help alleviate her loneliness. I also learned that she lived less than a mile away from me!

I was struck by my delight in discovering Denise, the flood of sincere gratitude and warmth I felt from her, and the feeling that I was sitting with a new friend. A sense of peace came to me, a stillness reflective of that still, small voice. And I knew that, whether it was instinct or the Spirit guiding me, I was right to follow it.

We talked for another 20 minutes before I really had to go. "Listen, Denise, give me a call if you need a ride to town. I come in at least twice a day, and since we live so close to each other, I'd be happy to swing by and pick you up."

As I drove away, I was smiling, not just at her and our budding friendship, but with deep thankfulness that I had heard—and listened to—that still, small voice.

BY ELAINE WRIGHT COLVIN

CALLED HOME

◈ ◈ ◈

◈ ◈ ◈ ◈

"Are you ready to go to heaven when the Lord calls you?"

◈ ◈ ◈ ◈

OUR SHUTTLE BUS sped through the darkness to Denver International Airport. My husband sat next to me, clutching my hand. I heard him swallow as he tried to suppress his tears. He whispered, "I can't believe we're doing this again."

Just nine months earlier we had sat on the same bus and raced through the same darkness to fly to Iowa before his father's imminent death. Mark's parents had attended Lenten services that night, and when the priest asked, "Are you ready to go to heaven when the Lord calls you?" Dad had responded with a confident, "Yes."

Four hours later he answered that call.

The stroke had been massive. The medical team had kept him on life support until Mark and I and his three sisters arrived. Then the respirator was discontinued. We stood together at his bedside and sang and prayed him into heaven. *"He will raise you up on eagles' wings…and hold you in the palm of His hand."*

Now, less than a year later, we were rushing to the bedside of Mark's mother. The doctors predicted that her congestive heart could beat only a few more days.

Her courage during the past few months had surprised us all. Even as a young woman, she'd been afraid to be alone. So when she insisted, after Dad's funeral, that she could live on her own, we were skeptical. Her health problems had increased over the years. Before he died, Dad had assumed responsibility for all the cooking, cleaning, shopping, and dispensing of Mom's numerous medications. It was with great hesitation and even greater faith that we supported her decision to stay alone in her home on a trial basis.

A visiting nurse and home health aide helped out once a week, but we were astounded by Mom's ability to care for herself. We marveled as she did many things only Dad had done for years. She persevered and succeeded even though we knew she was afraid—afraid of her diabetes, her ailing heart, the stairs inside and outside her house, and the increased crime in her neighborhood. She wore an emergency medical alarm button on her wrist and used the test button daily to ensure its performance. New security locks were installed, but we knew she still propped a folding chair in front of the door every night.

But all these fears were second to her greatest fear: dying. She had told us that many times. We guessed that fear was the only thing that had pulled her through several of her past critical illnesses. But, according to the doctor, nothing could pull her through this one.

We arrived at the hospital to find her sitting in a recliner. Her bright smile and joyful greeting were a stark contrast to her ashen color and shortness of breath. Mark and his sisters listened with Mom as the doctor explained that the medication being infused into her veins was the only thing keeping her ailing heart beating, and even that was short-term.

Respecting her fear, we supposed she would elect to continue the medical intervention to the end, which was predicted to be long and difficult.

◆ ◆ ◆ ◆

*Our voices
dimmed to a
whisper as we
listened to Mom
recite the verse
with conviction.
"Lo, though I
walk through the
valley of death, I
fear no evil…"*

◆ ◆ ◆ ◆

She slept most of the day, gasping from the continuous flow of oxygen. Her children sat in the adjoining waiting room discussing her terminal prognosis and how to support her decision. Her daughters recounted past conversations when Mom had spoken honestly about being afraid to die. Is there a way, we wondered, that we could give her permission to discontinue the medication without fostering her fear of death?

As the others talked about which words to use and anticipated her reaction to them, I peeked my head through the door to see if she was resting.

"Come in," she said. "I've been thinking. Is it okay with all of you kids if I stop all this stuff? I'm ready to go to heaven."

I summoned her children, and she repeated the question, then added, "Is it okay with you if I go now?"

"Yes, Mama, it is," they chorused through their tears.

She grinned. "Then let's get the show on the road! Dad's waiting! And what about Terry?" she asked, referring to her stillborn son from some 50 years before. "How old will he be when I see him in heaven? Will Dad be holding him in his arms, or will he be a grown man?"

Chuckles broke the sadness as we conceded that only God knew that answer—and soon, so would she.

We held hands around her bed and said the Lord's Prayer. The hospital chaplain appeared and suggested we pray the twenty-third Psalm. Our voices dimmed to a whisper as we listened to Mom recite the verse with conviction. "Lo, though I walk through the valley of death, I fear no evil…"

The nurse came and disconnected the technology that detained Mom on earth. Defying her diabetes, we celebrated with chocolate cake and tried to imagine her heavenly greeting. Would our late, great Aunt Hildie be playing the piano as Dad swept Mom into his arms for a waltz into heaven? Mom giggled with joyful anticipation.

The family teased each other and swapped animated stories and memories. Our hearts danced with a peaceful merriment.

The next day Mom phoned each of her grandchildren and told them good-bye. She ended each conversation with a cheerful, "See you in heaven!"

One of our daughters lamented, "Grandma, I think I found the man I'm going to marry. I so wanted you to meet him."

Mom reassured her. "I *will* see him in a few days, Honey."

On the second day, Mom slipped into a peaceful sleep, and we were all at her side when God called her home. Together, we bid her farewell and, joining hands, we sang, *"He has raised you up on eagles' wings…and holds you in the palm of His hand."*

BY LEANN THIEMAN

ONE WOMAN'S JOURNEY
From Darkness Into Light

◈ ◈ ◈

*N*EWSPAPER HEADLINES in South Florida for Thursday, December 22, 1988, carried a chilling account of a family abducted and held for ransom by three men armed with automatic weapons. The *Sun-Sentinel* in Fort Lauderdale ran: "$250,000 Kidnapping Ransom Paid, Thrift Chief's Family Freed From Car's Trunk." *The Miami Herald* said: "3 Hold Bank Chief and Family, Flee With Nearly $250,000."

Until that day, I hadn't given much thought to God and angels, I'm sorry to say. I was a workaholic mom, recently remarried, and preoccupied with climbing the corporate ladder, not the one to heaven. For the first 39 years of my life, God had been a security guard of sorts—someone I called upon only in times of need. I knew he was there, but I never really paid much attention to him. Today, God is…well, everything in my life. And I give thanks a thousand times a day. I wouldn't be here to tell you my story if it weren't for his angels who heard, and answered, my desperate cry.

That Tuesday in 1988, my new husband and I attended a routine dinner meeting with some clients. About 7:00 P.M., I called home to see if everything was all right and to tell my housekeeper we'd be home around 10:00. But when I spoke with her, she had a strange inflection in her voice that made me uneasy, even though she said everything was fine and told me not to worry. During dinner, I kept looking at my watch, anxious to get home. I could feel it—something just didn't sit right. The knot in my stomach got tighter as we approached the house. I nervously put the key in the front door and pushed it open. The first thing I saw was three men standing in our living room with guns pointed at us.

I turned and ran down the driveway, screaming. A man wearing a wig and carrying an automatic weapon came after me and pushed me down. "Shut up!" he ordered. "I won't hurt you, but you have to be quiet." He dragged me back inside. My husband was lying on the floor with his arms wrenched behind his back.

"Relax. We're not going to hurt you. We're just here to rob the bank," shouted one of the men.

"Where's my daughter?" I said, shaking and crying.

"Where's your purse?" he demanded.

After he took our cash, watches, and jewelry, again I begged, "Please, I have to go see my daughter." The lead man escorted me upstairs. She was safe, thank God, but my housekeeper looked mortified. I hugged them both in the dimly lit bedroom and tried to muffle my sobs. The men ordered my husband upstairs, too.

"In the morning, you will fill this duffel bag with cash," one of the men said, tossing it on the bed.

They called themselves "One," "Two," and "Three" and took turns standing guard throughout the night. We could hear the others snoring. They all wore wigs, sunglasses, and ridiculous-looking caps. Morning seemed forever away. I whispered to my daughter, "Let's go to sleep," and we huddled under the covers. My husband and our housekeeper were

For the first 39 years of my life, God had been a security guard of sorts—someone I called upon only in times of need. I knew he was there, but I never really paid much attention to him.

lying on the floor. I never closed my eyes. My mind was empty, nearly numb with fear.

It was still dark out at 5:30 A.M. when we were awakened and ordered outside.

"Now, you two, into the trunk," ordered One, waving and pointing with his gun.

"Oh, no, please don't put us in the trunk," I pleaded.

"Mommy, what are we doing?" my daughter asked in desperation.

"We're going to play hide-and-seek," I said nervously.

We curled up in a fetal position, and as the car began to move, I focused on the red glow of the taillights and the monotonous bumping of the tires. The only thing keeping me from going crazy was my daughter. We held each other tightly, and instinctively I started singing "Baa, Baa, Black Sheep," "The Itsy Bitsy Spider"…anything I could think of to help pretend this wasn't happening.

After being driven for what seemed like hours, the car stopped, doors slammed, and we heard muffled voices that got fainter and fainter. I was certain they had left us in the Everglades to die. The heat of the day was in full force, and the trunk felt like a sauna. We were rebreathing the same air, with very little oxygen, and I kept saying to myself: *God, I don't know if we can survive, I don't know if we can survive.* My chant became almost rhythmic as I rocked back and forth, with my daughter cradled against me.

By now, we were hungry. We were hot and cramped, and I didn't want us to fall asleep for fear we'd breathe carbon dioxide and never wake up. At some point, I gave up. "Let's close our eyes a little and take a nap," I whispered gently.

> ❖ ❖ ❖ ❖
>
> *My eyes were closed, yet I could see an incredible energy enveloping me. I was surrounded by gossamer beings of light, and though I could not see them, their voices sounded in my mind.*
>
> ❖ ❖ ❖ ❖

When I closed my eyes, I began to pray. And even though I don't remember ever memorizing the twenty-third Psalm, the words came clearly to my mind: *The Lord is my shepherd, I shall not want….*

When I finished the entire psalm, I told God that if it was my time to die, he could take me. I surrendered. But my daughter didn't deserve this. At that moment, I left my body through a tunnel of light. My eyes were closed, yet I could see an incredible energy enveloping me. I was surrounded by gossamer beings of light, and though I could not see them, their voices sounded in my mind. "Susie," they said, "there is nothing to be afraid of. You are protected by God and your angels." It gave me such a peaceful feeling, a feeling of pure love, that I immediately felt more at ease.

"Where am I?" I asked.

"It doesn't matter," they answered. "You are with God, and it's not your time. You are not going to die."

I felt like I was hovering, and I turned and could still see the car below, when they added, "You have much yet to do and to accomplish, and we are here with you."

In a flash, I was back in the trunk with a thud that frightened my daughter, and she started to cry.

Just then, I looked up and noticed a quarter-size hole in the trunk that I hadn't seen before. I said, "God is with us and the angels are with

us," even though my daughter clearly didn't understand what I was talking about.

Soon we were bathed in light. I could see the clear blue sky and some telephone wires, so I knew we were in town and not in the Everglades. I wanted to make sure I wasn't going crazy, so I asked my daughter, "Can you see the hole and the sky and feel the fresh air?" "Yes, Mommy," she said. "Where did it come from?"

"It's from God and the angels he sent to protect us," I said, kissing her hair and rocking back and forth. I knew then that we would be safe because someone or something heavenly had intervened.

A short while later, we were rescued by a group of police officers, my husband, and bank officials. It was a moment of rebirth, literally.

When some of the confusion surrounding the scene settled, I turned to look at the trunk that had nearly become our coffin. I saw tiny dents, but I couldn't find the quarter-size opening. It was no longer there.

Had we only imagined it? Or had we truly been saved by the hand of God?

I don't have any proof, of course. But what I've learned over the last ten years is that when science and logic and reality have no good explanation for something, that's when faith takes over.

My life is different now. I am different. My world has been inextricably altered, although nothing's changed except the way I look at it. I wouldn't wish the experience that transformed my existence on anyone. Yet, for me, it has been a gift, a blessing, and I wouldn't change it.

If it took this to bring the awakening of God into my heart, than it was worth it. I don't want to mislead you—it wasn't a magical, overnight

What I've learned over the last ten years is that when science and logic and reality have no good explanation for something, that's when faith takes over.

transformation. It took time. I struggled with the emotional aftermath of post-traumatic stress disorder and fought the fear, paranoia, and depression that threatened to consume me. I didn't immediately recognize the gift I'd been given, nor did I understand why. Those questions formed a long and arduous journey. But the answers took many forms and brought me to where I am today.

About the only thing I would change if it were up to me would be those headlines in the papers. They should have read: "God Sends Angels From Heaven to Rescue Kidnap Victims" or maybe "Heavenly Intervention Saves Mother and Child." But then, those kinds of headlines belong on supermarket tabloids. Who believes those kinds of stories anyway, right?

BY SUSIE LEVAN, AS TOLD TO M. L. PESSOA

THE NEHEMIAH PROJECT

❖ ❖ ❖

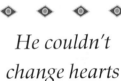*IRENS WAILED* in the night, echoing through the community of Jellico, Tennessee. Flames crackled and roared, leaping far into the dark sky, casting flickering shadows across the scene of devastation. Yet another church had been destroyed by flames, swelling the list of church-burnings that had occurred throughout the nation. There wasn't much anyone could do. The small building crumbled and collapsed, completely burned to the ground.

It wasn't the first church to burn. It wouldn't be the last. But for the close-knit African American congregation of the First Baptist Church of Jellico, it was their only church, and losing it hurt them all. Their little church had been there a long time, and now it was gone.

They joined forces to start all over again, knowing the work would be hard and lengthy. Some of the parishioners borrowed on their homes to help out, and many worked with their own hands to help rebuild what flames had so swiftly destroyed. But the work progressed slowly. Gradually, the frame and the roof went up, and the congregation rejoiced. But there were still no bathrooms, no plumbing, and no interior walls. So much hard work lay before them.

Meanwhile, in another state, Tom and Mary Hayden had been watching the nightly news, which was mostly bad news, as usual. Over the years they had seen too much footage of devastation and destruction, watching clip after clip of churches burned to the ground through the

❖ ❖ ❖ ❖

He couldn't change hearts that were filled with hate and bigotry. But he had to do something, …

❖ ❖ ❖ ❖

flames of ignorance. Tom hated seeing so many decent people left with smoldering ruins where once they had worshiped together. He'd had enough!

Mary turned to him as they watched and asked, "What are you going to do about it?"

What, indeed? What could one person do? He knew he couldn't stop the church burnings. He couldn't change the news reports. He couldn't change hearts that were filled with hate and bigotry. But he had to do something, and so he began calling around in search of something he could do to make a difference. He soon found Jellico, with its small, faithful congregation, working away at restoring their church. Tom contacted Pastor Gerald Littlejohn, and thus the Nehemiah Project began.

As often as he could, Tom drove the two hours to get to Jellico. He brought hammers, nails, and whatever tools he could find, and he brought as many helpers as he could round up, too. All kinds of people helped out, giving up their weekend plans to work long hours on the new church building. They constructed the stage where the minister would speak each Sunday. They hired experts to do the bulldozing and bricklaying. They worked on insulation. They put up walls and set new floors.

Every month Tom gathered his work crew. They were not always the same people, but there were always enough for a couple teams. They came from many different backgrounds and from different churches and beliefs. They worked in a variety of professions—there were salesmen, students, professors, engineers, librarians, doctors, computer programmers, and others. Tom brought his own plumber to help out, and a retired carpenter pitched in to donate his expertise. A full-time builder showed up with his own group of 15 willing assistants.

Campus Crusade for Christ sent a group. A pastor from Columbia, visiting the United States for a while, also showed up to help. A couple of missionaries on home leave drove down. One young student wanted to help, so she went out and bought herself a brand-new hammer and joined the work crews. Men from a university football team were also anxious to do their part.

Everyone took turns bringing food. And the congregation in Jellico joined the volunteers for meals and a visit, eating, singing, and praying together after they did their work.

Not everyone understood Tom's Nehemiah Project at first. Some people couldn't quite make sense of his desire to reach out to others no matter who or where those "others" might be. Not everyone felt friendly at first, and a few people were downright suspicious. Some of Jellico's residents looked at Tom and his friends as upper-class do-gooders who would perform a moment of charity in order to believe they were good people and then go back to their nice, comfortable homes and lives. But, after a while, attitudes changed. Resistance melted away as, month after month, Tom and his workers faithfully drove for two hours to get there, worked all day, then wearily headed home again.

Perhaps Tom's project touched hearts and set an example of what people can do for one another if they care and want to make a difference.

… its gates have been burned with fire. Come, let us rebuild the wall of Jerusalem, and we will no longer be in disgrace.
—Nehemiah 2:17

Tom named his project for the book of Nehemiah, thinking of chapter 2, verse 17: "…its gates have been burned with fire. Come, let us rebuild…." That's what Tom and his helpers did, counting on chapter 6, verse 9: "Now, therefore, O God, strengthen my hands."

The work was hard and required long hours. But perhaps Tom understood that the ultimate goal was not just to rebuild a church that had burned down. The Nehemiah Project also helped to build a bridge between people, between hearts, between spirits. Together, they built something no fire could ever destroy.

BY KAREN LEET

IS ANYTHING TOO SMALL FOR GOD?

❖ ❖ ❖

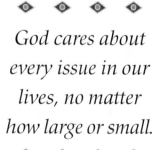

God cares about every issue in our lives, no matter how large or small.

S CHILDREN, we eagerly approach God with all our concerns, not stopping to contemplate how "important" they are. But as we get older, we start to wonder if the "little things" in our lives are really worth God's time.

When I'm faced with a crisis, I like to look back to two childhood incidents. To me, they illustrate God's caring nature and his willingness to answer our prayers, whether our troubles are big or small.

When I was five years old, there was a fire in the forest behind our home. At such a young age, it seemed to me as though the flames were coming dangerously close. Lying in bed that night, looking out at the stars, I prayed that the fire would not come near our house. I even asked God for a sign: If a certain star twinkled, everything would be all right. It did, and I drifted peacefully off to sleep.

The next morning, the fire had either burned itself out or been extinguished. That's when I learned my first lesson about answered prayer.

The second event happened when I was a teenager. After much discussion and a little arguing, I finally persuaded my father to let me get my ears pierced. As the holes in my ears healed, I searched for the perfect pair of earrings to wear, and I eventually decided on a pair of antique-looking beauties decorated with blue stones. Coming from such a poor family, I didn't have many pieces of jewelry, so I was quite proud of my new purchase.

One night I was out with some friends, riding around here and there, exploring city parks. When I got home, I realized I had lost one of my precious earrings. I was heartbroken, and I prayed that God would help me find it. It never occurred to me that God would not care about a piece of costume jewelry; all I knew was that he had answered my prayers before, and I hoped he would answer this one, too.

My friends and I had been to so many different places that night that finding a tiny earring seemed out of the question. Yet I asked God to show me where to look. That night I had a dream. I saw the earring lying on white gravel around the bleachers at a ballpark. There was only one place that fit this description, and the next day, I talked my friends into taking me there. Even though the area was large, by the grace of God I found my earring!

Throughout the years, these two examples of answered prayer have helped sustain my faith. If I'm faced with a problem, a struggle, or fear, I know I can share my troubles with God and ask him for his guidance and help.

As an adult, there are times when I don't want to bother God with a prayer that might seem unimportant. Then my mind goes back to the earring, which I now wear on a chain. To me, it serves as a reminder that God cares about every issue in our lives, no matter how large or small.

BY NAOMA COFFMAN

BLACKWATER SWAMP

◇ ◇ ◇

VERY CHRISTMAS, my husband, Tom, and I spend a month in Florida with his sister and her husband. We love challenges, adventures, and the thrill of exploring places that are not on everyone else's agenda. We find that being immersed in the nature that God has created and pushing ourselves to our human limits brings us closer to each other and closer to our Creator.

In Florida, it's sometimes hard to find unexplored and unpopulated areas we haven't already visited. For this trip, we decided to find a remote river in the wilderness that we could canoe.

A friend of ours said he had just the spot for us: Blackwater Swamp. He had canoed this area himself many years before and was awed by the beauty and seclusion of it. One section of the swamp was never used by tourists, and it sounded like just what we were looking for. The maximum time it would take us to get from bridge to bridge, after putting in the canoe, would be about three hours. We agreed that it seemed perfect.

On the day of our adventure, some of the family members stayed behind to prepare dinner, which was planned for 6:00. This would give us plenty of time to relax and enjoy ourselves on our excursion. Those who stayed at home to cook would meet us at the bridge around 5:00, so we'd have time to get cleaned up.

Five of us made the drive down to Blackwater Swamp. We all settled into our positions in the canoe and started paddling around 1:00.

The rivers we'd gone down before were always crystal clear, and we would enjoy watching the fishes that swam by us. But this waterway—the Blackwater Swamp—was different. It was so murky and dark, we couldn't see into it at all. Its name was obviously appropriate!

The scenery around the swamp was beautiful, though. A deer came down to the water's edge to drink, and we couldn't help but marvel at the abundance of wildlife all around us. God was truly in this place.

As we traveled deeper into the swamp, it seemed to be closing in on us. Trees were now laying across our path. The weight of all five of us made it impossible for our canoe to glide over the logs. We decided that the four women should get out and walk around the fallen trees, so Tom wouldn't have any trouble getting over them. This worked well and kept us moving along quickly. We ran carelessly from one place to another, getting in and out of the canoe as needed…until something changed all that.

I grabbed ahold of a tree to pull myself out of the canoe and went to place my foot on solid ground when my body froze in terror. Inches away from my foot, in striking position, was a huge rattle-snake. I screamed and fell back into the canoe. It was a miracle I wasn't bit-ten. From that point on, we all became much more cautious and aware of the dangers that were around us. At that moment, we realized we had no medical supplies or food, and we had no idea where we were or how long it would take us to reach the bridge. This was supposed to have been a short trip, but we'd already been gone three hours and could see no sign of civilization. It was clear that we would all have to rely on God to get us safely through this adventure.

My sister-in-law organized us into a single-file procession as we walked through the swamp. She was our lookout for snakes, since she was the most level-headed of the group. At one point, she told us to stay calm since there was a rattlesnake to our right. But her words fell on deaf ears. The rest of us screamed and took off running until we safely reached the canoe.

Tom was becoming concerned that we might not reach the bridge before dark. He was afraid we might take a wrong turn and end up getting lost. It was increasingly difficult to know where to go, since water was everywhere now. At times, the main path we were trying to follow blended in with the rest of the swamp. And although we'd been frightened by a number of snakes that day, we knew they weren't the only dangerous predators in these waters. Every now and then we heard a crashing sound on the shore beside us and tried not to think about what might be causing it. We were all getting anxious to be home.

With darkness rapidly approaching and the temperature starting to drop, we decided to put our situation completely in God's hands. We earnestly prayed that God would take us safely through these "troubled waters." I also asked God for a special favor. I told him how much it would mean to me if he could lower the logs enough for us to glide over them. That way, we wouldn't have to worry about getting out of the canoe. After we prayed, I felt a sense of peace flow through my body, and I knew that the Lord would answer our prayers.

After we prayed, I felt a sense of peace flow through my body, and I knew that the Lord would answer our prayers.

Darkness was setting in, and we were cold and hungry and tired. We'd been on that river for six hours now, fighting our way through foliage and trees. But after we stopped to pray, we didn't have to leave our canoe again. Every log we came to was submerged just enough for us to pass over it. Some trees were huge, and we had to feel our way along them until we could find an opening, but we always found one.

After what seemed like a lifetime of darkness and strange noises, we heard the sweetest sound of all: A car horn was blowing, and people were calling our names. We knew that we'd finally found the bridge with our beloved family members on it. But even after we first heard their voices, it took us another hour before we reached them, since the swamp was so full of twists and turns, we couldn't see where we were going.

As we finally approached the bridge, we were met by a forest ranger. He warned us to be careful getting out of the canoe because of the danger of rattlesnakes. We laughed and told him we knew all about them.

After nine hours on the swamp, with snakes, logs, darkness, and cold weather, we knew God was the one who had kept us safe and delivered us home through those troubled waters.

BY Kathy Giebell

LeAnn Thieman and Operation Babylift

◇ ◇ ◇

*I*T WAS ONE of those seemingly unimportant moments that ends up changing a life. When a young Iowa homemaker stopped at a bake sale to buy cupcakes, she set in motion the events that eventually led her to a rescue mission in war-torn Saigon.

In that most exotic place and dangerous time, the young woman was to both confront her worst nightmares and fulfill one of her deepest desires. The experience changed not only her life and the lives of the Vietnamese children she aided, but also the lives of many others with whom she has shared her story in the 23 years since.

At the time of her shopping trip, LeAnn Thieman was a 25-year-old part-time nurse and full-time mom, reared on a farm and now living in the idyllic small town of Iowa City, Iowa. The bake-sale booth piqued her interest because it was sponsored by Friends of the Children of Vietnam (FCVN). Impressed by the organization's mission to help raise money for orphanages in the war zone, LeAnn signed on as a volunteer. She eventually became FCVN's president, operating its Iowa headquarters out of her own basement.

"If there was anything I wasn't interested in, it was politics," LeAnn recalls. "I left politics out of it. The rightness or wrongness of the war was irrelevant to the welfare of the children."

LeAnn and her husband, Mark, had daughters who were then two and four. The couple decided they wanted to adopt a Vietnamese boy to complete their family. So LeAnn jumped at an opportunity that arose in February 1975 to go to Vietnam and escort six children back to the United States to preassigned homes of adoptive parents.

At the time, the trip sounded exciting but safe. "Mark and I had applied to adopt a son, and although we didn't expect that to happen for two or three years, I thought it might mean something to him someday to know that his mom had been to his homeland."

As the trip grew closer, LeAnn was riveted by news reports that the war was moving closer to Saigon. She began to lose her nerve. Her husband and family worried, too. "I often asked Mark what I should do. He'd say, 'Honey, you gotta do what you gotta do,' but I know the words 'Please don't go!' were screaming inside him."

LeAnn wavered until the last moment, terrified of leaving her little girls motherless. "On the morning I left, I heard a radio announcer say there was bombing within three miles of Saigon. I would not have gone if I hadn't had a powerful religious experience at church on Easter the day before. I went to church begging God for a sign that I did not have to go. Instead I was filled with courage and conviction. I had to go."

Accompanied by Carol Dey, another young homemaker and fellow volunteer with whom LeAnn remains close friends to this day, LeAnn stepped off the plane and was met by the overseas director of their organization, Cheri Clark. "Have you heard the news?" Cheri asked breathlessly. "President Ford has okayed a giant babylift. We're not taking out six children, we're taking 300 if we're lucky!"

◆ ◆ ◆ ◆

"I went to church begging God for a sign that I did not have to go. Instead I was filled with courage and conviction. I had to go."

◆ ◆ ◆ ◆

LeAnn recalls, "It was then I understood why I had said yes, and what the whole plan was." Still, when the group arrived, they found Saigon in a shocking and depressing state of chaos. "People were streaming down the streets, their possessions packed onto their backs, crowding around the embassy and the bank in droves, trying to leave the city. We could hear bombing in the distance. I was shocked to see sandbag fortresses in the middle of the street, with armed soldiers popping their heads out."

That sweltering night, LeAnn and her friend Carol slept on the balcony of a hotel, and they were terrified when awakened by gunshots. "I crawled on my belly, sure the Viet Cong were outside. But we soon discovered it was only young soldiers, some as young as 12, shooting at trash cans and rats."

They were also not prepared for the sight they saw at the FCVN Center, where hundreds of abandoned or orphaned babies cried and cooed from blankets on the floor. LeAnn recalls, "Most all of these children had been abandoned at birth. Many of them were of mixed race. In their culture, that was completely taboo. In Vietnam, you are who your father is. Some had been abandoned on the streets and others at birthing shacks throughout the city, where women would come, have babies, and leave them there for organizations such as ours to rescue."

FCVN worked feverishly to ready the children for what came to be known as "Operation Babylift." There was a hitch, however. Vietnamese government officials were annoyed with FCVN because of the unauthorized takeoff of a plane on which the organization had sent 150 children to San Francisco the day before. So the plane on which LeAnn and Carol

> *"I crawled on my belly, sure the Viet Cong were outside. But we soon discovered it was only young soldiers, some as young as 12, shooting at trash cans and rats."*

were scheduled to depart for the Philippines (the first leg of their long journey home) was bumped from the schedule until the government permitted it to leave—if it was allowed to leave at all.

Another organization would go first. LeAnn, angry about the change in schedule and anxious to leave Saigon, fought hard to get her organization's plane back into first place. When permission was denied, she had little choice but to help prepare 20 babies to be loaded onto a plane to Australia. While standing on the runway, she witnessed a plane of orphans heading to the United States crash shortly after takeoff, killing hundreds of babies and their escorts. The rumor at the time was that the plane had been shot down or sabotaged, although it was later learned that the plane was merely defective.

"When it crashed, so did I, and so did my faith," LeAnn says. "If they'd bomb that plane, they'd bomb ours. I went to the director and told her I had to quit and go home. She patiently and lovingly told me there were no other planes I could take and no other transportation out of Vietnam. The only way out was on Operation Babylift."

Matters weren't helped much when a sobbing LeAnn learned that an Associated Press reporter had awakened her husband back home in Iowa to ask if his wife was on the plane that had crashed. The reporter, who felt terrible about the incident, worked with other reporters across the continents to check on LeAnn's status and ultimately let Mark know she was okay.

The next day, FCVN's flight was cleared. LeAnn and the others frantically loaded the babies onto two gutted cargo jets under a makeshift arrangement: The babies were placed in 22 cardboard boxes, with a strap from one end of the plane to the other holding the uncovered boxes in place. Older children crowded onto long benches on the sides.

During the eight-hour flight on the first leg of the journey from Vietnam to the Philippines, "we just propped one bottle after another, burped like crazy, and changed hundreds of diapers." After a couple days in the Philippines, the rest of the trip home was easier. Each baby had its own seat, and military wives from the Air Force base helped out.

On top of the mission's success was an unexpected personal surprise for LeAnn—before flying out of Vietnam, Cheri had told her, "You and Mark are going to be assigned one of these children. You can wait and have a child assigned to you or you can go into that room over there and pick a child." Overjoyed, LeAnn "went in, and this little boy literally crawled across the floor and into my arms." The nine-month-old who filled her empty arms from the sea of babies at the crowded Saigon orphanage has grown into Mitchell, her 23-year-old son.

Today LeAnn, still a part-time nurse, is in demand as a writer and public speaker (she has written two books based on her experiences). Her message is that ordinary people can do extraordinary things if they listen to their hearts, trust their perceptions, and let themselves be guided by their higher power.

BY REBECCA CHRISTIAN

"We just propped one bottle after another, burped like crazy, and changed hundreds of diapers."

THE FORGIVING PLACE

❖ ❖ ❖

MPOSSIBLE! Not even after I blessed the meter maid who ticketed my car and the honking driver who wanted me to run through a red light by a school crossing. Not even after I blessed the IRS man who declared my home office a hall way and added penalties to esoteric taxes.

I'd come a long way on my spiritual journey, but blessing my ex-husband was out of the question. Maybe eternity would give me perspective. Meanwhile, I was more receptive to another one of St. Paul's tips for living the godly life: "If your enemies are hungry, feed them; if they are thirsty, give them something to drink; for by doing this you will heap burning coals on their heads" (Romans 12:20)—coals hot enough to melt my ex-husband's frozen heart.

No, I did not send him gourmet cheese for Christmas or sign him up for the Beer of the Month Club. The divorce settlement left me too broke to "heap burning coals on his head" in this way. It seemed rather tragic that I could not indulge my human torch fantasies by sending a gift of food or drink that he would not understand. I lay awake many nights, counting my ex-husband's various sins in case God was not keeping meticulous score.

Obviously, I started this spiritual journey with a handicap: righteous indignation. Okay, rage. Righteous rage. At first I'd felt I was the only woman in the world who had been betrayed. Then I learned there are

Bless those who persecute you; bless and do not curse them.
—Romans 12:14

tens of thousands. We fall into two camps: women cheated on who are over it, and women cheated on who never let anyone forget it. I was a "got over it" gal, and I bloomed in the praise of friends who admired my progress and courage. But I did not let God forget it. "Vengeance is mine," says the Lord, and I expected a front-row seat.

The spiritual journey progressed, but lessons in reconciliation were not part of my plan. I missed every sermon on forgiveness, either through laziness or divine intervention. I suspect God did not want one of his new recruits to leave church frothing at the mouth. Rage was something I simply carried with me. I never thought about how it might be slowing me down or keeping me from opening the doors to greener pastures, those places that have no room for the riffraff who carry nasty stuff in their hearts.

None of those thoughts were on my mind the day I revisited our old hometown. I found myself with a rental car and several hours between my last business appointment and my flight home. I had not wanted to go back there, but I couldn't tell my boss I was afraid the memories would break down my "got over it" facade and turn my friends' praise into pity.

The courthouse there seemed less imposing, my favorite department store had shrunk somehow, and the diner looked like just another greasy spoon. What was I doing in this dinky little town on such a glorious fall day? Pushing my luck! I hit the turn signal and headed for the cottage. The cottage on the river that contained 20 years of weekend memories. The hallowed ground of my happiness that he won in the divorce settlement. Too bad I loved it too much to burn it down.

It was Wednesday, so I knew he would not be there. Even so, I kept telling myself, "This is dumb." I remembered the hundreds of hot dogs we had roasted over the outdoor fireplace and how we would always watch the sun set over the river. Suddenly I was hungry, so I popped into the nearest grocery store. I drove on—no longer a vegetarian, apparently— with those plump hot dogs beside me. Formerly a drinker solely of healthy juice, I opened a root beer and guzzled my first soda in years.

The outdoor fireplace was still there, right where we had built it so we could cook and watch the river at the same time. The picnic table beside it did not look any older. The trees seemed the same height, and even the birds whistling above had not changed their tune. I felt like I had walked away last Sunday and was taking a midweek cottage break the way I used to do on late autumn days.

The woodpile was replenished, just like we left it every weekend, and the matches behind a chimney brick looked just like ones I had bought. I built a fire and remembered weeping here when my marriage fell apart. I threaded a hot dog on a wire hanger and went further back in time. I remembered a season of sacrifice—saving so we could buy a boat—and how we'd taught the kids to water ski. After the kids were asleep, we held hands and gazed at the stars from the boat, instead of on the beach, and laughed about how we'd come up in the world. I remembered a summer of sorrow when a child who should have been born in July arrived too early in the spring. My husband held my hand and didn't force me to talk about it. When I could not sleep, he walked along the beach with me and told me the names of the stars. We named one after the baby, and no one knows that name but me and him and God.

A blue jay answered my call and flew over the table, dropping a feather. Was this a message from animal heaven, where Thor was chasing rabbits again? I put the feather in my pocket.

"I'm sorry for all the pain I caused you....Do you think you can ever forgive me?" "Yes," someone said. I looked around. But that someone was me—and I meant it.

The hot dog sizzled, and my mouth began to water. I slathered on mustard and catsup and tasted the picnics of our lifetime. The table had looked so large when we built it, with just the two of us sitting there. By the time there were five of us, it was just the right size. I sat in my old spot, facing the fireplace with the river to my right. The laughter of my children was so near to me, I looked down on the beach to make sure no one was swimming beyond the dock. Whenever I whistled, our black lab, Thor, would come running with his tail wagging and shake river water all over me. I whistled, recalling how we had loved that dog from his naughty puppyhood to weathered old age, and how he had died in our arms. A blue jay answered my call and flew over the table, dropping a feather. Was this a message from animal heaven, where Thor was chasing rabbits again? I put the feather in my pocket.

The late afternoon was golden…the mosaic of sun on the table, a ray of light dancing across the river, the occasional maple leaf twirling down. Every thought I had was of our family—the humor, the love, and the brief squalls that did not swamp us, but just made us better swimmers.

I heard a motor and turned to see a car come down the dirt road, slow down, and then stop. My ex-husband got out. What was he doing here? He never came to the cabin on Wednesdays.

I sat up straight and smoothed my hair, putting on my "got over it" facade. Of all the people in the world, I especially needed him to believe I was okay with everything. But my stiffening soon felt unnecessary. I felt strange, but not vulnerable, and I greeted him easily. He seemed a little uncomfortable, but accepted my offer of a hot dog and began to roast it over the fire.

I passed him the mustard, knowing he never used catsup, and asked, "What are you doing here?"

He opened a root beer. "I don't know. I was sitting in my office and all of a sudden I thought of the cottage. I didn't plan to come here. Somehow, I just ended up here."

The silence did not seem awkward. There was nothing to say. From our separate benches, each leaning an elbow on the table, we watched the sun slide behind the hills across the river and withdraw its last ray from the sky. "I gotta go," he said, then paused. "I'm sorry for all the pain I caused you....Do you think you can ever forgive me?"

"Yes," someone said. I looked around. But that someone was me— and I meant it.

On the plane ride home I remembered the words of St. Paul. I had fed my enemy, given him drink, and not one single hair on his head had smoked. Somehow, that was okay with me. My rage had been unloosed from my heart, and I felt suddenly free. I pulled the feather out of my pocket and wondered how something so light and delicate could soar so high. I hoped my ex-husband was feeling as unencumbered as I was. Or maybe that was my prayer.

BY CAROL STIGGER

LESSONS OF LIFE

❖ ❖ ❖

*G*OD GRANT ME *the serenity to accept the things I cannot change, courage to change the things I can, and wisdom to know the difference.*

–ATTRIBUTED TO REINHOLD NEIBUHR

CLASS MEETS ON TUESDAY

❖ ❖ ❖

"DEATH IS AS NATURAL as life," said the professor. "It's part of the deal we made." The professor knew his life would end someday. In fact, he knew the year and the season. He faced this time realistically with no hope of a medical breakthrough or a miracle cure. But this is not a sad story. This is Morrie's story. He died several years ago, but thousands of people meet him every day in bookstores and libraries across the country.

Dr. Morrie Schwartz, professor of sociology, presented his final semester to a class of one, his former student Mitch Albom. Class met on Tuesdays in Morrie's home study until he could no longer sit up. Then, class was held in his bedroom. The subject was "the meaning of life," and Morrie had become an authority. "Once you learn how to die," he said, "you learn how to live."

The best teachers are those who teach not from theory, but from personal experience. An archaeology professor who has not been on a dig can give a credible description of an Etruscan clay pot. But without enduring weeks of toil and unexpected difficulties in a strange land to extract that clay pot, it is just an artifact, not a treasure. Morrie's deal with life included the experience of a long, painful, and frightening death. Enduring this ferocious struggle made him treasure his life even more.

Morrie loved to teach, and he loved to dance. In his sixties, he was still doing both with enthusiasm. Few people knew that the prominent

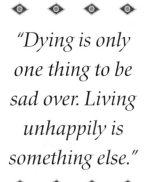

"Dying is only one thing to be sad over. Living unhappily is something else."

doctor of sociology spent every Wednesday night doing the lindy, the twist, the tango, a waltz—whatever the band was playing. Morrie also enjoyed swimming and long walks. He attributed his first few stumbles to fatigue, not unexpected in an elderly man who led such an active life.

Then, he fell down a flight of stairs and knew that something was seriously wrong. Many doctors and numerous tests later, Morrie learned he had amyotrophic lateral sclerosis (ALS), Lou Gehrig's disease. No cure has been found for this disease. No treatment slows its progress. Nerves die, often beginning with those that control the legs. The body slowly loses its ability to function. The certainty of becoming unable to walk and use his hands was bad enough, but Morrie knew he would also lose the ability to hold up his head, to chew, even to swallow. Finally he would draw one breath and, no matter how hard he tried, he would not be able to take another.

He was diagnosed in summer. By September, he was unable to drive and needed a cane to walk. He began the fall semester, but warned his students that he might not be there for the final exams. When winter arrived, he was still teaching and swimming, but he needed an aide to help him dress. He completed the semester, the last one he taught at the university, and then he went home. Death would be his final project. He would chart the journey between this life and whatever came next. He selected a student to share the journey with, one he had not seen in two decades.

Morrie was not as surprised as his student, Mitch, to discover that dying is all about living. Morrie had many visitors. Although healthy, many were unhappy. "Dying," Morrie told Mitch, "is only one thing to be sad over. Living unhappily is something else."

Morrie concluded that our culture does not teach us how to live. It does not ask the questions people need to consider in regard to how they are living their lives. Morrie asked Mitch four questions: Have you found someone to share your heart with? Are you giving to your community? Are you at peace with yourself? Are you trying to be as human as you can be?

Mitch did not answer. In the study of his frail teacher, who now had to be tied to sit up in his wheelchair, he remembered his old dreams of joining the Peace Corps, living in inspirational places, and never working just for the money. For ten years he had been living a fast-paced life, making a good income. He felt connected to his cell phone and computer, but not to nature or even to himself.

Mitch's pensive expression was all the encouragement Morrie needed to offer bold advice. "You have to be strong enough to say, 'If the culture doesn't work, don't buy it.' Create your own. Most people can't do it. They're more unhappy than I am right now."

Morrie stopped talking to resume eating a meal he had started 40 minutes earlier. His fingers shook. He could not press down hard with a knife or fork. He had to chew each bite to mush before swallowing or he would choke. The nerves in his tongue and lips were so impaired that food often slid out of his mouth.

Was the professor hinting that the very life Mitch was leading could become a fate worse than ALS?

Morrie did not put a positive spin on having to ring a little bell for help in turning his head or holding a tissue to his nose. Sometimes he couldn't make his hand grasp the bell and had to wait for what he needed until someone came in the room. "It's horrible to watch my body wilt away," he said. His grieving time was in the morning after passing through those slow dreamy moments when he felt healthy, eager to begin another active day. "I mourn what I've lost," he said. "I mourn the insidious way I am dying." Sometimes he cried. But always, he would stop feeling sorry for himself and concentrate on the joys the new day would bring: friends, good conversation, and the view outside his window. "I don't allow myself any more self-pity than that," he said.

Mitch thought about the healthy people he knew who spent days feeling sorry for themselves. If Morrie, who had so much to grieve, could put a limit on self-pity, why didn't they? And, more important, why didn't he?

Perhaps the measure of a successful life is how one defines "a perfect day." Mitch asked Morrie how—given good health—he would spend a perfect day. In Italy, maybe? Or having lunch with the President?

No. Morrie's perfect day began with exercise, sweet rolls and tea, a swim, then lunch with friends. In the afternoon, he would visit with more friends, one or two at a time, then take a walk to enjoy the trees, the sunset, and the sounds of the birds. Dinner would be pasta and duck. Then he would dance with many partners until he was exhausted. A deep, restful sleep was a last, but important, part of Morrie's perfect day.

Morrie had many such days throughout his life, days where nothing remarkable happened, like meeting the leader of the free world or walking through the Colosseum, but that were filled with activities and companions he treasured.

The final exam was held beside Morrie's bed. Morrie's skin was tight against his cheekbones. He was fighting for each breath and could barely

◆ ◆ ◆ ◆

"You have to be strong enough to say, 'If the culture doesn't work, don't buy it.' Create your own. Most people can't do it. They're more unhappy than I am right now."

◆ ◆ ◆ ◆

whisper. Yet, he mustered the strength to say, "This…is how…we say…goodbye." He rested awhile and then spoke again with a tear in the corner of each eye. "Love…you."

Mitch kissed his teacher on the cheek. Morrie raised his eyebrows slightly at the sight of Mitch's tears and said his last words to his student, "Okay, then."

Morrie did not believe in working just for a paycheck, yet he worked with Mitch until his last week on their book, *Tuesdays with Morrie*. The advance money helped to pay for special assistance that made his last months more comfortable. Morrie died before the book was published.

Morrie had invited a small group of friends to his "living funeral" shortly after he was confined to a wheelchair. He had wanted to enjoy the elegies and tributes to his life. Some guests cried. Some laughed. One woman read a poem that talked about his "ageless heart" and called him a "tender sequoia." Morrie laughed and cried along with his friends and called his funeral a "rousing success."

Morrie's second funeral was "graduation day." Mitch watched as his teacher's ashes were buried in a pastoral scene with trees, a hill, and a pond that was home to many quacking ducks. He remembered Morrie saying, "You talk, I'll listen." Before the service was over, he had his first imaginary conversation with Morrie. He knew his teacher was listening and would always be listening. What Morrie had told him was true: "Death ends a life, not a relationship."

It felt natural to talk to Morrie at his funeral. After all, it was Tuesday. Time for class.

BY CAROL STIGGER

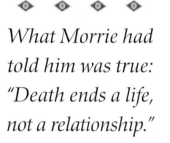

What Morrie had told him was true: "Death ends a life, not a relationship."

BUCK'S TENDER SIDE

◇ ◇ ◇

*H*E'S THE ONE, I thought, staring into the eyes of the medium-sized white dog at the local animal shelter. He looked like he was part white shepherd and part Lab. There was something sad about those eyes—something pleading—even more so than the other dogs we had seen that afternoon.

Days before I'd said, "You've got to be kidding," when my husband, Steve, suggested that we get another dog. Having one dog was hard enough for me. Since I'd been bitten as a child, I had developed a fear and, at times, a hatred of dogs. I had seen them as mean, even wondering at times why God had put them on the earth. Certainly not for us to have as pets. Maybe they should just stay in the wild.

Our first dog, a seemingly too-closely bred dalmatian, had confirmed my "dogs are mean" theory by biting my five-year-old's ear. We gave the dalmatian away to a man with no children, and we now had Shadow, a beagle-shepherd mix. I felt proud of myself for adjusting to life with a dog in the house. But two dogs? I went to the animal shelter under protest.

Yet there, sitting across from me, was Buck. He wasn't barking like the other dogs. He was just looking intently at me, and I felt drawn to him. We took him outside with Shadow, whom we had brought along.

The two dogs played a game of doggy tag, and Buck seemed to like our daughters, too, vigorously wagging his tail while they petted him.

I carefully studied the information card and discovered that the previous owners couldn't keep Buck anymore because he had dug his way out of their fenced yard. We would have to keep him on a leash. "We can break him of his digging habit," my husband said optimistically.

Buck arrived at our house and seemed excited about his new surroundings. He chased our two younger cats, but didn't seem to want to hurt them. He barked at Katy, our "queen" cat, who hissed at him from the safety of her perch on the back of the couch. But Buck's message seemed to be, "Can't we play and be friends?"

In the days ahead we found out that the trouble with Buck wasn't just about digging, although he did enjoy that. We noticed that Buck had certain fears. If he was startled while sleeping, he would awaken in an attack mode. If we moved quickly, he would lash out at us, opening his mouth and putting his teeth on us but never drawing blood. Still, it was disconcerting.

He also seemed obsessed with shoes—especially the athletic kind. Whenever someone would come into the house wearing white athletic shoes, Buck would charge at the shoes as if he were furious at them.

We also discovered he was afraid of baseball caps. One day, my nephew came into the house wearing one, and Buck lunged at him and tried to take the hat off with his mouth. At first glance, it looked as if he was going for my nephew's face.

Buck cowered when my girls played with a baseball bat in the yard. From Buck's behavior, we surmised that someone who wore athletic shoes and a baseball cap had kicked Buck and possibly even hit him with a baseball bat or at least threatened him with one. This someone also could have kicked him when he was sleeping.

I considered giving Buck away, but who would take a dog that was so aggressive? I had known people who put a dog like Buck down because they thought he was dangerous. But he didn't seem dangerous to us—only scared. Yet, what if he snapped?

I discovered when Buck wasn't scared, he was very loving. He cuddled up close whenever he got the chance, and he always seemed eager for tender words. When I would say, "Oh, Shadow, you're such a sweet doggie," Buck would come running from the other room and try to push Shadow out of the way and get close to me, with a "say-that-to-me" body wag. Even now, he loves to be petted and pushes his snout under any available hand to get some affection. When I lie on the bed, he often jumps up and snuggles with me. Our other dog is much more aloof, so it's great to have a dog who craves our love and attention.

As we contemplated the possibility of giving up on Buck in his early days with us because of his negative behavior, I thought of the people I know who had been abused in childhood. They, too, have behaviors rooted in fear. They overreact to situations because they're afraid of being hurt again. I had to admit that sometimes I wanted to give up on my relationships with them because of their snapping at me. Yet, as with Buck, they had never really hurt me—they had just startled me with their defensiveness.

As time went on, I learned things about Buck and about people who have been abused. My first impulse when Buck switched to his fear mode

The more we show love to him, the less fearful he is and the more he trusts us.

Through Buck, I've learned to have compassion for and patience with people who have been hurt and who demonstrate fear.

was to scold him. That didn't help at all, but only made him more afraid. I soon learned that talking tenderly to him calms him down right away. Early on when I would take him out at night, fear would suddenly overtake him, and he would walk around cautiously as if something or someone was going to attack him at any moment. When he was in this mood, he refused to "do his duty." I would get so frustrated that I would shout, "Bucky, will you just go already?" Soon I learned that if I said in a loving way, "Oh, Bucky, you are such a good boy," he would snap out of his fear mode. I've found that this works for people, too. If they are afraid and acting strange because of it, lashing out at them doesn't help. Yet if I build them up and say something kind, reminding them that I love them, many times the fear goes away.

Buck loves other dogs and always seems eager to greet them on our walks. Even if another dog is aggressive toward him, Buck rarely fights back. He just stands there or moves back a few steps. We do some dog-sitting, and Buck loves the "company." He also enjoys playing with Shadow, his "little sister." They run from room to room and then stop to wrestle on the carpet. Buck is never too rough with her, even though she's smaller. They seem to have an understanding. One or the other of them will snort during their wrestling matches and that means, "I've had enough" or "Let's rest a minute."

His tenderness toward anyone who is hurting has also really struck me. One day at the vet, some boarding dogs were outside howling and Buck let out sympathy howls in unison with them while I paid the bill. Then when we got outside, he went and licked each dog that was chained up. He's the same way when he knows that anyone in the house is upset.

He wants to make sure he offers comfort—either with a concerned look, a lick, or a snuggle. Sometimes he just lies down on the floor nearby as if he is guarding the one who is upset. We have had a recovering drug addict and, on a couple occasions, a psychiatric patient live at our house short-term. At first I was afraid of what Buck might do. But he seemed especially loving toward these guests.

We've had Buck for over five years now, and the longer we have him, the more we understand him. The more we show love to him, the less fearful he is and the more he trusts us. Through Buck, I've learned to have compassion for and patience with people who have been hurt and who demonstrate fear. I've also realized God is that way toward us. Now I know why God made dogs—at least I know why he gave Buck to us: to give us some lessons in loving.

BY ELAINE CREASMAN

UNEXPECTED PLEASURES

❖ ❖ ❖

*H*OW MANY OF US are stuck in a routine? We do the same things, in the same order, day after day after day. To stray from that means to wander into the unknown, to risk chaos, and maybe even to have an adventure! When events happen that are not within our control, we feel powerless, even helpless. Of course, I can't speak for everyone, but this is certainly how I feel. But I've learned that sometimes, in the midst of a frustrating day, the most simple gesture—a mere smile or show of concern—can make all the difference in the world.

My husband and I recently had a baby boy. He is our first child and the light of our lives. When my maternity leave was almost over, I decided to go back to the office to prepare for my return to work. This was my first morning away from my son. Needless to say, I felt anxious.

Considering how long I had been gone from the office, though, not too much had changed. The same people were waiting at the same bus stop at the same time in the morning. The same driver was on the bus. The man at the newsstand where I buy my paper was still there, listening to the same radio station. There is a certain comfort in that kind of pre-dictability. But on this particular day, I was impatient. I wanted to get home to my son.

Finally the morning ended, and it was time for me to go! I left my downtown job eager to get home to my husband and son. It seemed as if

I was waiting an eternity just to cross the street to the bus stop. My real impatience began there. Would the traffic light ever change? Imagine my dismay when the bus flew though a yellow light just as the pedestrian signal flashed "walk." I knew it would be another half-hour until the next bus arrived, and a 20-minute ride from there.

If I start walking now, I thought, *I could be home sooner than if I wait for the next bus.* I hadn't brought my sneakers along, so I knew what I was in for. Despite my uncomfortable footwear, I started walking.

The shortcut through the park seemed like a good idea. Maybe I could cut out five or ten minutes. *Besides,* I thought, *my feet hurt from my hard-soled shoes hitting the sidewalk. The grass might be easier to walk on.*

The sky was gray and it looked like rain. Hopefully the storm would hold out until I was home. The dreary weather seemed to reflect my mood—I was angry and sad at the same time. Muttering expletives in my mind, I thought, *If the traffic light had changed just five seconds sooner, I would be home by now.*

My inner monologue so occupied me that I barely noticed the beauty that surrounded me. Springtime shrubs flourished in glorious bloom. Forsythias were beaming yellow all around. Thousands of tulips in carefully planted beds were in bud, ready to erupt in a riot of color. I did note pessimistically to myself that the squirrels had made a meal of one entire bed, where only decapitated stems and leaves stood.

Suddenly, from out of nowhere came two unleashed dogs—a large rottweiler and a bulldog—who began to circle around me. My heart skipped a beat as I thought, *Maybe I should have waited for that bus.*

Their owner called them away. I released a sigh and desperately prayed, *Please just let me get home!*

Just blocks from my house, a truck slowed down alongside the curb where I was walking. The men inside it were calling out things I cannot repeat to civilized readers. Eyes straight ahead, I ignored them and continued to walk. They finally gave up and drove away.

I crossed the street almost in tears. I was tired and my feet hurt. It was about to rain. I had missed my bus. Strangers and dogs had pestered me. All I wanted was to hold my son.

Then something happened I won't soon forget. A grandfatherly man slowed down his car, opened his window, and asked if I was all right.

"Were those fellas in that truck bothering you?" he asked.

I noticed over his shoulder that there were rosary beads hanging on his rearview mirror. Funny, I had just prayed the rosary the night before.

"I'm fine," I assured him.

He drove off and, just one block away from home, I felt my burden lighten. In front of the Ronald McDonald House, three children, no more than eight years old, were running a hot cocoa stand.

"Would you like some hot cocoa?" the little boy asked me. "It's free."

"I would love some," I answered, noticing a little donation box. In it were one nickel and one dollar.

The littlest girl bashfully added, "It's free, but you can make a donation if you want, maybe a nickel or something."

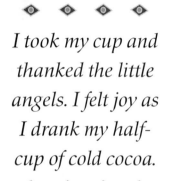

I took my cup and thanked the little angels. I felt joy as I drank my half-cup of cold cocoa.

"Oh, I'm sorry, I don't have a nickel," I replied. "Would you take a dollar?"

"Sure!" she said, accepting my offering.

The third child, obviously the oldest, poured my cocoa but quickly realized there was only enough for half a cup! She stared into the empty thermos, blushing. It was adorable the way the three of them looked at each other, all thinking, "Oops!" Obviously they had been sipping some cocoa.

"We gotta make some more," whispered the boy, hoping I couldn't hear him.

I took my cup and thanked the little angels. I felt joy as I drank my half-cup of cold cocoa. Waiting at home for me were my wonderful husband and beautiful son. I have a family. I have love. My cup is full.

BY GINA M. SMITH

MR. VANBROOKHOVEN:
A Life Well-Lived
◆ ◆ ◆

EVERY WEEK I look forward to opening our local newspaper to read refreshing, direct letters to the editor from someone named Henry VanBrookhoven. The letters are satirical with a dry wit, taking pot-shots at everything from high taxes to the death penalty. Mr. Van-Brookhoven has spoken out against aspects of educational structure, politics, the parole system, car insurance, and the lack of God in our schools. He has written letters to presidents, governors, senators, and congresspeople. A strong proponent of a good work ethic, he believes that "we now have too much confusion in high places."

After years of savoring his letters, my curiosity got the best of me. I decided I wanted to meet this prolific gentlemen, and when I called him, he agreed to meet me.

His name hangs in his yard from an old water pump; there's also a sign stating that all his visitors bring him happiness—some by coming and some by going. Henry VanBrookhoven has resided in this five-room house in Mahwah, New Jersey, since 1934. This man with twinkling eyes and a wild shock of gray hair, his face mapped in wrinkles, sees joy in all facets of his life. And his joys are legion!

The youngest of nine children, Henry received his working papers at age 14 and did just what the papers gave him permission to do. It was the Depression era, and his family moved from Passaic,

New Jersey, where they had owned—and lost—a carpet-weaving business, to Mahwah, a place that offered the opportunity to raise chickens and sell a few eggs. Henry had a small route where he sold vegetables. He also worked as a stone mason (the face of his little home shows his skill), and he drove a truck for a while.

Henry participated in the liberation of Czechoslovakia (along with the rest of the 16th Armored Division) in 1945. When other GIs received their two-week passes and set out for exotic beaches after the liberation of Europe, Henry headed for the Cordon Bleu Cooking School in Paris. He honed his culinary skills throughout his marriage and would "give his wife a break" at a time when a man in the kitchen was unheard of.

Cornelia, his wife of 44 years, died in 1983. VanBrookhoven began writing poetry then, his first piece written after her death from cancer. She was "a beautiful person, inside and out. I miss her terribly," he says. He lovingly shows a picture of her donning a large sunbonnet—"her poem" is attached to the photo.

Henry is a prolific writer, using different formats depending on what he wants to express. His letters to the editor allow him an outlet for his opinions, which are mostly common sense based on his spiritual foundation. He also writes poetry for his church bulletin. Amazingly, Henry VanBrookhoven is immortalized in the National Library of Poetry with his piece entitled "The Power of Love" (about Cornelia). Another poem, "More Precious Than Gold," was purchased by a greeting card company and used for anniversary cards.

Now an 83-year-old "philosopher," Henry leads a Spartan existence. But for him, his comfortable home holds more beauty than any of the

Now an 83-year-old "philosopher," Henry leads a Spartan existence. But for him, his comfortable home holds more beauty than any of the mansions that surround it.

mansions that surround it. His house is furnished with many pieces created by his own hands; the tables and chests are worn by age and use. He thought about subdividing his property, but, according to the town government, it wasn't large enough to parcel. So, out of his small pension, he continues to pay his $3,000 tax bill—a bill that used to be $76.

VanBrookhoven plants dahlia bulbs every spring and faithfully digs them up in the fall. He makes hundreds of bouquets from his flower garden and then gives them to the sick or his church. The waitresses at the Stateline Diner and the checkout clerks at the A&P have also received his nosegays. "They brighten my days, so why shouldn't I brighten theirs?" he asks. Ever generous, Henry also makes dollhouses, completely furnished, for children who might not otherwise receive a holiday gift.

This octogenarian, who is impressively healthy and fit, has to walk backward down his basement stairs because of knee injuries sustained during World War II. His basement has a concrete floor that he mixed and poured by hand in 1959; it also contains a sump pump that might have worked years ago and large signs that Henry puts out on special occasions, like the one for Valentine's Day reminding people to "love someone today." He proudly shows photos of his dollhouses, something he considers a labor of love. As he holds the tiny handcarved pieces of furniture in his large palm, I can't help but notice the stark contrast of dainty dollhouse furniture to the leathery hand of the master builder.

Henry never misses a Sunday service and takes great pride in the precious respect his spiritual community gives him. His prized possessions, in addition to his photos, are an old Dutch prayer book and the history of his family, which dates back to the 1600s. He loves to talk about his roots, his siblings, his son, and his granddaughter. He knows that all the good things in his life are from above—and he is very comfortable with that thought. VanBrookhoven proudly states that he continues to tithe ten percent of his simple funds, and he prays standing up because his knees just do not obey him anymore.

A first-generation Dutch American, Henry speaks proudly of the time he served in the war under Patton. He prides himself in missing only four elections during his lifetime—it seems the Germans kept him too busy to vote. He spent the war in Minsk, Munich, Kelheim, and Passau; he then went on to Czechoslovakia. (Little did he imagine that he would be returning to Plzen, Czechoslovakia, in 1995 to honor the fiftieth anniversary of Plzen's liberation.)

VanBrookhoven is unique, direct, and God-fearing. He writes everything in longhand, sometimes in duplicate. He does not own a dishwasher, an electric typewriter, or an answering machine. He knows that simplicity is a choice. He also knows that he is thankful to his Maker for putting food on the table and a roof over his head.

Henry considers his memories treasures to share. He speaks lovingly of his surroundings, his family, and his church. He is absolutely convinced that they enrich him far more than he enriches them. When all is said and done, I suppose Mr. VanBrookhoven is entitled to his opinions—after all, he has been writing them for years, based on his deeply held beliefs and personal experiences, without even a second thought or any desire for recognition. His life has been extraordinarily full and, undoubtedly, well-lived.

BY ELIZABETH TOOLE

He knows that simplicity is a choice. He also knows that he is thankful to his Maker for putting food on the table and a roof over his head.

DANDELION DREAMS

◈ ◈ ◈

Growing up in Atlanta, I lived in a fancy neighborhood. It was enclosed by a black wrought-iron fence, and at the front gate there was a little gazebo where a gentleman in a green uniform checked people in and out. Everybody's yards were mowed the same height; flowers were chosen, arranged, and judged against a high standard; shrubs were kept pruned just so; and leaves were raked, bagged, and hauled away almost before they hit the ground by a service that came to the neighborhood in an old pickup truck.

People driving along our street used to slow down and stare at the sweep of our manicured lawn and the carefully designed and tended flowers. We had the prize yard. It was like a painting, someone once told my mother. She was pleased because she did most of the work herself. She spent hours on her hands and knees, planting, weeding, trimming, and fertilizing.

It was us, her kids—Toby, Patsy, and me—who caused our mother "more trouble than a swarm of grasshoppers," as she used to say. It was probably true, because sometimes we forgot her rules and took shortcuts across the yard. That was a no-no. So was having a dog, which would surely leave spots on the grass and dig up Mother's prize flowers. We couldn't have a swing set either, or play ball on the lawn—both would cause the same unthinkable damage: ruts and bare spots on the pristine canvas of green.

Mother wasn't really that fussy indoors; it was just something about her yard. "First appearances, you know. A yard makes a statement," she said. "People can tell right away what kind of family lives here."

This is why we couldn't believe our eyes when we came home from school one spring day and there, in our driveway, was a man unloading square logs from a truck. The kind of logs that were used to build playsets! The deliveryman even left a fireman's pole, swings, monkey bars, and a climbing net on our front lawn.

"It's high time there was some playing done in this fancy yard," said Mother.

We tried to be careful, but by the time the playset was built, the bare spots were already forming in the yard from where we'd started playing with the logs even before they were put up.

"Not to worry," Mother assured us, setting a picnic table on the velvety green grass within easy distance of the playset. It was so she could watch us and eat at the same time, she said. "And what about all the food we're likely to spill?" she asked. "Wouldn't a dog help clean up crumbs and crusts?"

We all went to the animal shelter and brought home a brown-and-white, long-tailed hound that immediately went to sleep under Mother's prize-winning dahlias, breaking some of the new stems.

"Not to worry," Mother said. "Puppies need their rest. After all, these are the 'dog days' of summer." Our father thought this was so funny, he laughed until he cried.

People were still driving past our house; sometimes they slowed, even stopped. But now they were saying to one another, "What is going on?"

"We're making a statement," Mother told one lady bold enough to ask, "about the kind of family that lives here. Let people talk, but tell them to send their kids on over."

"We're making a statement," Mother told one lady bold enough to ask, "about the kind of family that lives here. Let people talk, but tell them to send their kids on over," she said, hanging a rope swing from the oak tree out back to seal her invitation.

"How about getting up a game of football with some of the neighborhood kids?" Mother asked us that fall.

There was, she pointed out, plenty of room in the front yard. The azalea bushes could mark the goal lines at one end, and the lilies could mark the other.

"Not to worry," she said when she saw the ruts and bare spots between the two. My father bought her a chaise lounge so she could rest while she watched us play. Sometimes the dog laid there with her, both of them snoozing while screaming kids scored touchdowns in the gathering dusk.

It was useless to fertilize the lawn the next spring—it looked hopelessly ragged. First base here, third base there, home plate out by the roses…we had become the designated neighborhood playground.

Now when people slowed to stare, they did so with raised eyebrows. My mother just waved from the chaise lounge where she spent most of her time now, laughing about the wonderful family that lived here and the statement it was making.

Drawn like moths to flame, the neighborhood children continued to come, knowing that they were not nuisances, but welcome guests at the party of childhood thrown by my mother in her last year of life. She understood that life comes and goes faster than the fluff on a dandelion.

BY MARGARET ANNE HUFFMAN

84 ◆ *WHISPERS FROM HEAVEN*

FRANK McCOURT'S LOVE OF LEARNING

◈ ◈ ◈

OST OF AUTHOR Frank McCourt's childhood was spent in a ramshackle, flea-infested cottage at the end of the road in Limerick, Ireland. (He was born and had lived in Brooklyn for four years before his parents returned to their home in Ireland in 1934.) In rainy seasons, sewage flowed from the neighborhood outhouse next door, making it impossible to live on the first floor. Before deserting his family completely, McCourt's alcoholic father drank up the few dollars they managed to earn or beg. The family survived on fried bread and tea, with the occasional boiled pig's head to celebrate Christmas. As a young boy, McCourt watched three of his younger siblings die of disease and malnutrition.

In spite of his late father's obvious faults, McCourt speaks of him with great tenderness, calling him the "perfect father," were it not for the alcoholism that kept the family in abject poverty. When he was home and sober, McCourt senior's tales of Cuchulain, the mythical Irish hero, fascinated his son and helped weave the bond between them. In a touching paragraph in his memoirs, the younger McCourt writes, "I know [Dad] drinks the dole money and Mam is desperate and has to beg…and ask for credit…but I don't want to back away from him. How can I do that when I'm up with him early every morning with the whole world asleep?

◈ ◈ ◈ ◈

His simple message to the kids was this: Respect yourselves. Get past your anger. Realize the importance of your lives and "go forth," as he had done.

◈ ◈ ◈ ◈

He lights the fire and makes the tea and sings to himself or reads the paper to me in a whisper that won't wake up the rest of the family. My father in the morning is still mine....[He is] my real father."

Despite the family's hardships—or perhaps to escape them—McCourt became an avid reader, often sitting on the curb under a streetlight because their cottage had no electricity. Recuperating from a severe bout of typhoid in the hospital—where he slept on clean sheets, ate three meals a day, and was bathed regularly for the first time in his life—ten-year-old McCourt discovered Shakespeare while reading a history book loaned to him by a fellow patient. "If I had a whole book of Shakespeare, they could keep me in the hospital for a year," he later wrote in his memoirs.

In grade school McCourt was a gifted student, but he abandoned the classroom at age 14 to deliver telegrams—a desperate effort to escape the poverty he had suffered since birth. Five years later, when he had finally assembled enough money for passage, McCourt set sail for the land of plenty: America.

When he first discovered the New York Public Library, McCourt walked hesitantly past the two forbidding lions that grace its entrance, fearful that the staff would prove equally dour. Back in Limerick, he recalls, librarians treated him like a "barbarian," protecting their precious books from his dirty hands and unwashed clothes.

The library's grand marble staircase led to the third-floor reference room, where McCourt timidly fingered the endless rows of index cards. To borrow a book, he learned, he would have to go to the lending library in the basement. To his surprise, he was readily offered a library card and invited to begin borrowing volumes that very same day. To celebrate,

McCourt remembers, he proudly displayed his four books as he rode home on the upper level of a double-decker bus, a very special treat.

After repeated trips to this newfound literary treasure trove, a librarian suggested to McCourt that he visit the bookstores along lower Fourth Avenue; every spare penny McCourt had went into the coffers of those booksellers. But pennies were hard to come by for a young immigrant earning a scant $32 a week. McCourt often walked to the stores to save the cost of a round-trip subway ride. That dime represented almost half the price of a used paperback.

After several failed jobs and a stint in the U.S. Army, McCourt turned to stevedoring. Living in the South Bronx, he commuted to Manhattan's Hudson River docks each day to unload huge sides of mutton, pork, and beef. It was June, and the papers were filled with reports of college graduations and commencement addresses, which McCourt read voraciously while riding the subway to work. He dreamed of the day when he, too, would be dressed in a cap and gown, holding a diploma in his hand. But that hardly seemed possible since he had never even graduated from high school. He did have the benefit of the GI Bill, however, and that made the dream more achievable, at least financially.

"Teaching was the most exalted profession I could imagine."

What McCourt really wanted was to be a teacher. According to McCourt, "Teaching was the most exalted profession I could imagine." But without a college degree, he would have no choice but to remain on the docks. So the plucky 23-year-old decided to try his luck with the admissions officers of New York University. He relied on his own engaging personality and on the blarney instilled in him by his father, a superb storyteller. Arguing that the impressive collection of books he had read prepared him to enter college, McCourt persuaded the school to admit him on probation for one year. He attended classes during the day and continued working on the docks at night.

It was at NYU that McCourt first uncapped his pen to write about his squalid childhood…memories of what it was like to sleep with five others in a single flea-ridden bed, to wear shoes with no soles, to search for bits of coal along the roadway to heat the teakettle, to consider the gnawing pain of hunger an everyday occurrence, and to live as a social outcast.

McCourt was surprised at the reaction of fellow students, who found his tale both tragic and entertaining. But not even their positive response gave McCourt the courage to write the story of his youth. It continued to haunt him throughout the 30 years he taught in the New York City school system.

In the classroom, McCourt revealed many things about his childhood in an effort to stimulate his students to write about their own experiences. He credits that sharing with helping him overcome the sense of shame he had felt about his poverty as well as his belief that his life's tale would hold no appeal for the reading public. Earlier, he had written individual vignettes and even attempted a novel based on his days in Limerick, but he found that it did not work because the voices were false. The story was so gripping and so meaningful to him that any fictional interpretation would defile those haunting memories.

It wasn't until he retired and reflected on his years as a teacher that McCourt turned seriously to the task of writing his life story. That was in 1994. McCourt's memoir, *Angela's Ashes*, has sold almost two million

His lifelong mission has been to help young people recognize the power of education.

copies, reached the top of *The New York Times'* nonfiction best-seller list, and captured the National Book Critics Circle Award, in addition to the 1997 Pulitzer prize for biography.

As an impoverished teenager, McCourt had talked of coming to the United States, where he would consciously commit a crime in order to be sent to an American prison because it was warm and provided three meals a day. As an adult, McCourt has never forgotten what he's achieved through his dedication to learning. His lifelong mission has been to help young people recognize the power of education.

For Frank McCourt, learning was a marvelous thing: It turned a seemingly unattainable dream into reality. It rescued him and gave him wings. Education and determination molded a scruffy, impoverished boy from the slums of Ireland into the winner of a Pulitzer prize, America's most coveted literary recognition.

Only a few days after the announcement of his Pulitzer, McCourt traveled to a depressed Long Island community to speak at its high school. His simple message to the kids was this: Respect yourselves. Get past your anger. Realize the importance of your lives and "go forth," as he had done.

Coming from a man whose childhood made theirs seem almost luxurious, that message had meaning, real meaning, to these disadvantaged teenagers. Tears brimmed in the speaker's eyes as the kids stomped their feet and cheered. Not only had they enjoyed hearing McCourt's stories, they had learned from them, too.

BY **CHARLES JACOBS**

THE REUNION

◈ ◈ ◈

NO ONE I KNOW is quite ready to admit that a 40-year high school reunion is just around the corner. It's frightening to think that we only remotely resemble our former selves. I look at pictures of myself as a teen and stare in disbelief. Was I ever that young and fresh-faced? On the inside I feel quite the same, for the most part. I have the same youthful enthusiasm about life and look forward to each day with eagerness. But reality sets in when I catch a glimpse of myself in the mirror. Could that really be me? I don't think I recognize that person. Surely, I must look as young as I feel! Alas, this is not the case.

I reached a new plateau in my life when I received an invitation to my 40-year class reunion. My first instinct was to toss it and pretend that it never existed. After all, no one would remember me anyway. Five- or ten-year reunions were filled with hours of fun and lighthearted banter. Everyone still looked about the same—if not better—and the captain of the football team and most popular cheerleader could still be easily recognized. No red-faced apologies there.

Now let's take a look at my impending reunion. Just remembering the first names and some of the events we shared as classmates could be traumatic! The inevitable "HELLO, MY NAME IS…" stickers don't help much since most of us wear bifocals or, at the very least, reading glasses. Everyone knows you must be within inches of those little white badges before the name can be read. Then, as beads of perspiration begin to form on our temples, we are expected to remember everything about that person in less than 60 seconds.

I clutched the invitation in my trembling hand and moaned, "Another reunion already? I can't possibly have been out of school that long! Can it be true?" As I peered anxiously into my unfriendly mirror, I got my answer.

Yes, it was true, and now I'd have to meet my former classmates once again—in a well-lit room, no less! I would quietly note that they, too, had aged a bit and hope I could remain in the shadows lest they observed that old father time had also visited me. I began to realize that poor memory and weakened eyesight were just the tip of the iceberg. What about all those wrinkles and bulges? I was determined to make my old body look its best even if it killed me in the process.

I decided a new outfit was a must. The initial excitement of shopping, however, ended almost as quickly as it had begun. As soon as I was able to squeeze into an outfit, I anxiously looked into the glaring, oversized mirror. The figure staring back at me was definitely not the one I had envisioned when the dress was on the hanger. When did I put on those extra pounds, and where did all those new lines on my face come from? I was told once that they were laugh lines, but I saw nothing funny about the theory at that moment.

As I struggled to get out of the tight, trendy dress, I tearfully admitted that I would have to resort to a "comfortable" outfit. Ugh! That meant only one thing: something loose and boxy, with plenty of room for expansion in case I spent too much time at the dessert table.

After a long, hard day of shopping, I trudged home, wishing I had spent the afternoon in the grocery store instead. At least there weren't any mirrors there! Would anyone at my reunion care that I had given birth to three beautiful children and earned each roll on my stomach? I was sure they wouldn't. It seemed pointless to keep up this battle with my outer self, since it was making my inner self feel awful.

As the reunion drew closer, I began to reevaluate the importance I was placing on my outward appearance. I began to realize that my faith, my family, and inner peace were far more important than the size or style of my dress. I had been making the outside packaging overshadow the real person within. After all, I reasoned, wasn't it more significant to show an interest in old friends, to really listen to them and let them know that I cared about who they had become?

I shed the foolish pride I had been harboring and knew that getting older brought with it a fair amount of wisdom, experience, and compassion. And if it brought with it a few pounds, a new line here and there, and a few gray hairs, then I would wear them proudly.

The big night finally arrived. As I strolled into the reunion hall, I had a new, healthy attitude. I was no longer interested in recapturing my youth by squeezing into an uncomfortable outfit. Everyone else there was my age anyway, so there was no need to feel the self-inflicted pressure of growing older. I spotted a few thinning heads and some thickened waistlines, and I heard myself telling my old classmates how great they looked. And they did! There is something to be said for mature men who are not looking for the fountain of youth and for women who are not interested in stumbling around in high heels and tight sweaters. They exude a self-

I began to realize that my faith, my family, and inner peace were far more important than the size or style of my dress.

assurance that is extremely appealing and can only come with the experience of living on this great earth for many decades.

Everyone in the room had floated in the same aging boat as I, and we did not feel the sense of competition sometimes found at high school reunions. There was warm camaraderie, a recollection of fond memories, and a comfortable, relaxed atmosphere.

I was surprised as I listened in on the animated conversation between the men who had been on the football team. They were in a world of their own as they reminisced about many of the games they had played. They recalled opposing teams, memorable scores, and funny stories of bus rides. Their fond high school memories would never be forgotten. As I walked around and listened in on some of the discussions, I looked at my former classmates somewhat differently. To me, they hadn't aged at all. They had a youthful excitement in their voices as they recalled high school antics, and their recollections were extremely detailed. I was impressed! We were all teenagers once again, if only for an evening.

Our graduating class was small to begin with, and since that time many dear friends have passed on. I felt privileged to have had the opportunity to enjoy the rest of my high school buddies that night. Sharing teenage experiences was wonderful, and the evening was a huge success, even for this old gal.

I am so grateful that I did not let my own insecure feelings take over, and place outward appearance ahead of what was really important— enjoying the company of old friends. Why, I felt so self-assured, I boldly walked up to the dessert table—twice!

BY ELEANOR M. BEHMAN

◈ ◈ ◈ ◈

*We were all teen-
agers once again,
if only for an
evening.*

◈ ◈ ◈ ◈

HOW POPPY LOST HIS ONLY SUIT

◈ ◈ ◈

WHEN I WAS GROWING UP, I got to spend a lot of time with my father's paternal grandparents. Deeply devoted to each other, they told the kind of stories you appreciate only as you get older.

My great-grandmother's father had fought in the Civil War. My great-grandfather had grown up on his parents' farm outside Cincinnati. Both their families had come to the area around Cincinnati right after the Revolutionary War. Throughout their life together, they conducted a "discussion" about which side of the family had done the most for the people in the area, which had fought in more wars, which had donated the most to churches, schools, etc.

I have a picture of them from early in their marriage. They're standing, with the rest of my great-grandfather's family (the family called him Poppy) outside the house. My great-grandmother (who the family called Mommy) sits in front with Poppy's parents. Poppy stands in the back, with his brothers and the hired hands. Each of them holds one of the two children they had by then, having faith that life would improve.

As a young man, Poppy became known in southern Ohio as a great speaker about religious topics. A local church was impressed enough with his oratory skills and knowledge of the Bible that they took up several special collections. They then put Poppy through college so he could become a minister. (This all took place about 100 years ago.)

He and Mommy were delighted when he was assigned to his first "circuit" in southern Indiana. This allowed them to leave Poppy's parents' farm and move to their own home.

This first home was so isolated, there were no roads leading to it. They had to take a riverboat to move there. However, Poppy's new position would provide a little extra work (and income) while they farmed and raised the four children they would eventually have.

There were three churches in his circuit. Poppy used a horse to get between churches and was known as a "circuit rider." It was not an easy profession, but circuit riders were responsible for spreading religious teachings in many isolated areas.

Mommy, meanwhile, pinched a penny every way she could and made things do and redo. Though she always had a little gift for a new neighbor, she had a reputation for being extremely frugal.

Throughout her life, her favorite gift to newlywed couples was a jar of bacon grease. "You need bacon grease to cook," she would announce. "And I presume you don't have any yet."

She always made her own clothes and the children's as well. And she made Poppy's first suit—at that time, the only suit he had. Until her dying day, Mommy talked about how she worked and slaved over that first suit to get it to fit Poppy just right. The measurements, the sewing, the fittings, the cutting—Mommy pored over every inch of that suit to make sure it turned out perfect.

Throughout her life, her favorite gift to newlywed couples was a jar of bacon grease. "You need bacon grease to cook," she would announce. "And I presume you don't have any yet."

Just when Mommy had finished the precious suit, a rider came from a distant village. A former member of one of his churches had died. Poppy remembered the deceased man clearly. He was not particularly well regarded by the community, but he'd been loved by his family.

"Could you get to the home in time to preach the funeral tomorrow morning?" asked the rider.

Poppy could if he left immediately. He packed his only suit, prepared his horse, and rode through a good portion of the night. He was dressed in what he considered his "riding clothes." If he encountered trouble (like a flooded creek or a muddy path), his packed-up suit would still be clean and ready for "preaching."

He arrived at the home of the deceased at daybreak. The funeral would be at the home, but instead of being held in the morning, it had been delayed until the afternoon. As was the custom then, the body of the deceased was in the parlor, and the local ladies were going to dress him. There seemed to be only one problem: They couldn't find any "decent" clothing.

Poppy was invited to sleep in a spare bed until an hour before the funeral. Meanwhile, his suit was hung up to remove the wrinkles. An hour before the funeral, he was awakened by calls from the parlor.

"Reverend Miller! Come and see! We found the most beautiful suit." The ladies talked all at once. "This will make the family feel so much better. We have no idea why we didn't see it before!"

Not wanting to meet the ladies in his long underwear, Poppy wandered from room to room. Where had his suit gone? "I'll be right there, ladies. Just let me find my suit."

He came across his riding clothes, but not his suit. He could not find the suit Mommy had put so much love and care into. He found the hired hand who had taken the suit earlier. "It was right here," confirmed the young man. He had hung it exactly where Poppy was looking.

Suddenly, Poppy heard the ladies in the parlor again. They were talking to an early arrival. "You know he never spent any money on clothes, but look—we found this nice suit, hanging like it was waiting for him."

Poppy dressed in his riding clothes and went to the parlor to confirm his suspicions. The ladies greeted him, "You know, Reverend Miller, we were worried. His clothes were rather old and ragged. The family loved him very much, and they want to show the community how much they loved him. They wanted him to look respectable before he was buried, and that didn't seem possible, until we found this suit."

There it was, Poppy's only suit. His only suit that Mommy had worked on for so long, with so much love and care. After complimenting the ladies on how nice the body looked, my great-grandfather returned to the bed where he had slept, sat down, and weighed his options.

At home was a formidable and frugal woman. (Many years later, when she was in her 80s, a teenager made the mistake of trying to steal Mommy's purse. She beat him to the ground and sat on him until the police officers arrived.) In front of him was a family who loved their husband and father, a family who wanted their loved one to look respectable in the eyes of the community.

He had ridden through the night to be with a family who wanted to say good-bye to their husband and father. This family wanted to be comforted by him and the community.

"They wanted him to look respectable before he was buried, and that didn't seem possible, until we found this suit."

In Poppy's eyes, there was only one solution. He had to leave the suit where it was. It would be six feet under soon, but Mommy would understand. At least, he hoped she would understand.

According to family legend, Poppy delivered one of the most moving orations ever preached in Indiana that day. Before or since, the story goes, there has rarely been an oration delivered with such emotion. The listeners cried, they laughed, they shouted, and they sang.

Among the family, however, there is some debate over whether Poppy was preaching about the loss of the deceased or the loss of his suit.

It doesn't really matter. The family of the dead man was greatly comforted, and the community saw that the family loved him. After Poppy left, returning home to face Mommy, the community continued to comfort the grieving family.

Poppy lost his only suit that day. Many times since I've thought about that story and tried to follow his example: Choose what is right, not what is easy. Lead by example, not just by words. Or, as they say now, "Don't just talk the talk, walk the walk."

Could I have done what Poppy did that day? I'm not sure. Mommy was certainly intimidating at any age. But Poppy had other suits later, so they must have come to some kind of agreement, eventually. Mommy had faith and believed in doing the right thing, just like Poppy did.

That's what I try to remember when making a decision: Have faith. With faith you are never wrong. More poorly dressed, perhaps, but definitely not wrong.

BY DEBORAH J. MILLER

Poppy lost his only suit that day. Many times since I've thought about that story and tried to follow his example: Choose what is right, not what is easy. Lead by example, not just by words.

ENJOYING THE BEAUTY

❖ ❖ ❖

"AS ANYONE FROM out of state?" the tour guide asked.

I raised my hand.

"Where are you from?"

"Florida," I said. *Where there is nothing to compare with the beauty of autumn we're seeing here*, I felt like adding.

While we waited for our afternoon tour to begin, I asked the lady next to me where she lived. "St. Charles," she said, adding, "You know, I was here last week, and the leaves were stupendous on this tour."

"They look lovely today," I said. "And it's a perfect day."

The temperature was around 74, the sun shone brightly, and a gentle breeze rustled the leaves. I felt like a tourist who had just discovered a gold mine. Although I had passed this arboretum every day on my way to junior college years before, I had taken it all for granted back then.

As the bus started on the tour, the lady next to me said, "I notice a lot of leaves have fallen since last week. That tour was just perfect."

"That's nice," I said and turned my attention to the tour guide, who told us about Mr. Morton, the owner of the Morton Salt company, and how he decided to build an estate here, which eventually became the Morton Arboretum.

As we rode along, the tour guide pointed out different trees and clusters of trees. "Oohs" and "aahs" came out of my mouth each time I turned to where she pointed.

❖ ❖ ❖ ❖

As we rode along, the tour guide pointed out different trees and clusters of trees. "Oohs" and "aahs" came out of my mouth each time I turned to where she pointed.

❖ ❖ ❖ ❖

"Look over there," the lady next to me said. "See that cluster of bare trees? Those had gorgeous red leaves on them last week. It was absolutely breathtaking."

I looked at the bare trees and tried hard not to think about what I had missed.

What about the breathtaking view on our right? I felt like asking.

"Yes, those leaves last week were so beautiful—this is nothing compared to last week," Ms. Party Pooper rambled on.

Well, it's something for me. I haven't seen autumn leaves in years, I argued in my mind. I looked around again to see another beautiful grove of trees.

Soon we were deep in the forest. My neighbor told me again and again how the beauty of these leaves wasn't nearly as wonderful as those she'd seen last week. Then suddenly we were surrounded by yellow; sugar maples stretched in every direction. The tour guide stopped the bus so we could get a better look.

"Wow! This is great," I said, enraptured by the gorgeous colors surrounding us. My neighbor was silent, but only for a moment.

"This tour guide is not as good as last week's," she whispered.

After we were out of the deep forest, the tour guide said, "On the right, you'll see the brilliant red of the bush referred to as 'the burning bush.'"

"They're not as brilliant as they were last week," my pesky neighbor added.

I wasn't here last week, so they look brilliant to me! I felt like yelling.

In the midst of my anger at this woman for wrecking my nature adventure, a gentle whisper came to my soul: *You act like her sometimes.*

As I compared the beauty of these trees to the wonder of God's love, I saw how many times I acted like this lady.

As I compared the beauty of these trees to the wonder of God's love, I saw how many times I acted like this lady, keeping my mind on what God had done in the past and comparing those miracles, vainly, to present negative events—the bare trees in my life. I thought about how when I became too focused on the pressures of life, I no longer sensed God's presence, his amazing love for me, and the beautiful things he had brought into my life.

At first I felt pretty bad about getting "stuck" next to that lady. I've since concluded that maybe she was a widow who felt she was in a "bare trees" phase of her life. Now when I think back to that day, I'm thankful for her. Through her, God showed me there will always be obstacles to sensing his love, the beauty of the world, and the beauty of people around me—obstacles that come both from within and from outside myself.

Today I choose to look beyond bare trees and see the beauty all around me.

BY ELAINE CREASMAN

GUIDING BY INSTINCT, LEADING BY LOVE

❖ ❖ ❖

Bill's intuitive response to his canine friend shows that love and kindness are two fundamentals that don't need to be taught.

S HELPING OTHERS an intuitive response, or is it taught by example or training? Consider the story of Bill and Ben, a couple of Jack Russell terriers who now live a comfortable life in the English seaside town of Brighton. Not long ago, both dogs were strays who wound up in desperate trouble in the village of Averley. When shelter owner Michael Feiler responded to a distress call, he found two terrified little dogs. One was cowering, with a blood-streaked face and obvious eye injuries; the other was barking hysterically and guarding his injured companion. Using all of his charm—and a few of the dog biscuits he usually carries with him—Feiler managed to calm the dogs, and he wasted no time in getting the injured one to a veterinarian. When the vet realized it was impossible to save the dog's eyes, they were removed, and the eyelids were sutured shut. Soon Ben, as the blind dog came to be known, grew healthy enough to be released to the shelter and reunited with the other pup, who by this time was called Bill.

Then, intuitively, Bill began to do what it usually takes seeing eye dogs months of practice to accomplish: He became a guide dog for his newly sightless friend. Ben seemed to understand exactly what he was supposed to do. He would grab a mouthful of the scruff of Bill's neck, and in this way the two walked a slow circuit around the shelter's yard.

They kept this up until Ben knew exactly where to find food, water, the doorway, and a place to sleep.

Feiler had never seen anything like it, and word of the amazing little dogs quickly spread. After footage of their routine appeared on TV, five-thousand people offered to adopt the pair. Bill and Ben were eventually placed with an elderly couple in Brighton who already had a female Jack Russell terrier named Rosie. The dogs' new home, however, was a three-bedroom townhouse with a two-tiered garden. Would this pose a problem for sight-impaired Ben? Not with the help of his good buddy Bill, who offered the scruff of his neck, a nudge here, and a tug there, until Ben became familiar with his new surroundings.

Like Bill, there are special dogs across the country who help others in small but profound ways every day: They guide the sight-impaired through crowded streets, help people in wheelchairs go shopping, alert hearing-impaired parents to a baby's cries. While assistance dogs are specially trained to respond in certain ways, Bill's intuitive response to his canine friend shows that love and kindness are two fundamentals that don't need to be taught.

Bill and Ben now sleep snuggled together like young pups, and the bond between them is stronger than ever thanks to Bill's loving, intuitive responsiveness. A story that might have ended tragically had a happy outcome instead, testifying to the innate goodness of all who helped and reminding us of the special power of friendship.

BY DIANA THRIFT

FOR THEIRS IS THE KINGDOM OF HEAVEN

❖ ❖ ❖

*L*IKE A ROW OF JAGGED teeth, a picket fence surrounded the wooden shack of the orphanage in Kingston, Jamaica. A welcoming committee of ragged toddlers ran through the doorway. Damien raised his arms, commanding, "Up! Up!" as his soggy diaper drooped lower. He wiggled in my arms, tugging at my earring, pointing to a skinny mutt. "Rufus," he said. "Rfff! RFFF!" Then he pointed at me.

"Carol," I replied, wondering if he would call me "Mommy" instead. Isn't that what orphans want—a mother? I put him down. He tugged me past the miniature circus of toddlers and dog.

Inside, the walls were bare wood, the floor was hard-packed earth, and the windows had no glass or screens. Lying on split, faded mats or propped in rusty wheelchairs were the children who could not go outside. A woman toting a stack of stained, plastic bowls and a steaming kettle of beans jerked her chin, inviting me into the dining room.

Children grabbed bowls with no hesitation, spoons, or manners. Laughter and sunlight filled the sweltering room as the children enjoyed their communal feast, sharing bowls, food dripping from chins, beans scooped from the floor. Damien held a fistful of mushy beans to my mouth.

Soon, an aide swept the lunch leavings outside. The children marched like new recruits to the kitchen sink, where the laundress stood

❖ ❖ ❖ ❖

Laughter and sunlight filled the sweltering room as the children enjoyed their communal feast.

❖ ❖ ❖ ❖

all day washing orphaned children, bedding, and clothes. The lone flush toilet, which sat behind a plywood partition, was too high to be of use. The children who were out of diapers were given plastic pots instead. The laundress scrubbed hands and faces, changed clothes, and dashed behind the partition to empty out the pots. I wanted to help, but there seemed no way to penetrate this dance of the barefoot, turbaned "earth mother" and her twirling, squatting, grunting, giggling partners.

Damien wiggled out of his wet diaper and streaked out the back door. He motioned for me to follow him out and then in again. We galloped through the day room past the children in wheelchairs being fed from one spoon by an aide, to a quiet dormitory.

A maze of iron cots was the nursery for 32 children. The infants slept in fruit crates and cardboard boxes. In one corner, broken bedsprings and slats were piled higher than the window. Thin shafts of sunlight streamed through the skeletal bedding waiting to be repaired, not junked. In Jamaica, it seemed only people were junked, with the occasional child salvaged and recycled into humanity.

Damien commanded attention away from the larger picture by flinging a sheet over a cot. I tucked in one of the corners, but before I could make the bed, Damien jumped on it to the twang of rusty springs.

A baby slept in a fruit crate on a trestle table. Sun blanketed the child's naked back. I whispered, "Ssh." Damien leapt from the bed and shook the crate. "A-ME! A-ME!" he hollered and ran away.

I patted the sleeping child, Amy; too big, I thought, for this infant bed. I wondered at her lack of response in this riotous place. The laundress came in laden with sheets. "Amy," she said, shaking her head. "Found last month in the dump. She don't laugh. Don't cry. Opens eyes. That be all."

I picked Amy up, the warm stone body of her. Her eyes opened, and I waited for them to focus. But Amy's gaze was empty. Enraged shrieks would encourage me, even vomit spewing on my arm—any emotion or action to help me liken this child to something other than a lumpen weight growing heavier and colder, now that I had removed her from the puddle of sun.

The laundress asked me to take Amy to the day room. I sat her in a little wheelchair. She looked old enough to sit up, even to walk, although blinking her eyelids seemed an act of gravity, not physiology. I searched for something to secure her, then realized what the rags were for, tied like streamers to the rusty steel arms. I tied her to the chair and pushed it to the row of wheelchairs flanking a mat where more children were lying, audience to Damien and friends.

Their game was ring-around-the-rosy, with a cockroach for a "rosy." The children held hands and tumbled down, cheering the roach in its flight for the wall. Damien, diapered again, stomped on the roach and picked the pieces from his toes. A boy in a wheelchair scrunched his palsied face into a smile.

Seated alone on a plastic bench was a tall, emaciated child in a garish pink party dress with a torn lace collar. Her posture was queenly, her smile gentle around teeth too large for her face. She smiled at me, welcoming me like she was the hostess of this melee, but she was just a child, barefoot and party-frocked.

"Who is she?" I asked the aide now spooning mashed beans into Amy, who drooled them out again.

"Donna," she said, scraping mush from Amy's chin. "Found last week, naked in a shack, starved and raped," her voice wavered in watery ripples. "Someone carried her here. Can't keep food down. We're making her comfortable, but…," she shrugged.

I noticed the bulge of Donna's abdomen, distorting the pink folds of her skirt.

"She's not…pregnant? She doesn't even have breasts!"

"Starved. That's how it looks like, don't you know?"

I didn't know. Ashamed of my ignorance, I asked Donna if I could sit beside her. She nodded yes and moved to one side of the bench, making room for me. I put my arm around her, and her head drooped to my chest. She felt warm and feather-light. I stroked her forehead; it felt feverish. "How are you feeling?" I asked.

"Not bad." Her voice was musical and sweet. She nestled closer and her sigh was a light puff on my neck. Damien plopped beside me, demanding my other arm. His juggling did not disturb Donna or my own quiet peace in holding her. Across the room, Amy's open eyes were pointed right at us, but there was no connection. She would have held the same stare on a train wreck or a closed curtain.

I rubbed Donna's abdomen. It was bloated, but hard—stony as Amy's stare; the muscles spasmed from hip to hip. Her neck was supple, and her back bent gracefully until she lay with her head in my lap. Amy's stare faded from my consciousness. Only Donna remained, and with each breath she became more my own child. I envisioned her tucked into bed

Donna taught me that birth children and children of the heart stir the same instincts.

in my sewing room, the room with the dormer windows and morning sun. I would buy her a canopied bed and cover her with the *Little Women* quilt my mother had made. I would feed her soup with a silver spoon and sing her lullabies.

Donna sat up and said she needed to go to the bathroom. She held onto my arm and walked like a frail, old woman behind the plywood partition. She sat down and smiled at me, daintily holding her skirt, stroking the rayon folds as if she had never before touched smooth fabric.

Next, she wanted water. "Little bit," she said seriously, holding her thumb and forefinger an inch apart. I poured it into a glass.

An aide said, "She's always thirsty, but it usually comes up again." Donna sipped slowly, then asked to go outside. In the dusty yard, she seated herself on a stool and tilted her face to the sun. She seemed to be in another place, one that was wholly her own. I watched Damien catch a butterfly. I waited for him to tear off its wings, but he stroked it gently, raised his hand, and watched it fly away.

I looked to see if Donna had witnessed the small drama. She was looking at me, sadly now. Bile ran down her chin and on the lace of her charity-box dress.

I leaned forward to help her, but my feet would not move. Her eyes asked nothing of me except that I acknowledge her mortality. I tried for a very long time before I was able to move and do for her what a mother would do, including promising her a new, clean party dress.

I bought the dress in Miami, a yellow one for the sunshine she had enjoyed that day. I sent the dress by Federal Express so she would not have to wonder long if I would keep my promise.

◆   ◆   ◆   ◆

I bought the dress in Miami, a yellow one for the sunshine she had enjoyed that day. I sent the dress by Federal Express so she would not have to wonder long if I would keep my promise.

◆   ◆   ◆   ◆

Donna died before her new dress arrived.

Through the years, she has been a gentle memory. Those tender hours in which she let me mother her healed my private pain that I could not have more children of my own. But Donna taught me that birth children and children of the heart stir the same instincts. I believe she knows I kept my promise to her. I believe she knows I keep my promise each time I reach out to a child who needs mothering, if only for a moment.

BY CAROL STIGGER

LESSONS FROM GRANDMOTHER ROSE

◈ ◈ ◈

"WASTE NOT, WANT NOT," Grandmother Rose always used to say, "for a little can be a lot."

She and Grandpa George used to live in a little four-room house they built in the midst of an unkempt five-acre orchard in central Indiana. When they moved in, the fruit trees needed some care to get back up to speed, but Grandmother Rose could always see the value in time well spent. After a few years, the overhauled orchard was producing plump peaches and crisp apples again, and they were in business.

The years passed fruitfully. Rose and George enjoyed a peaceful life on their Midwestern oasis. Gradually, Grandmother Rose started a few small gardens to complement the orchard, and she always got a pretty good yield. Corn, tomatoes, watermelons, and cucumbers sprouted healthily out of that country dirt.

After Grandpa passed away, Grandmother Rose continued to manage the orchard and keep up the gardens, still drawing customers for miles. Holding true to her maxim, she never wasted anything, even making corncob jelly and strangely tasty watermelon rind pickles. The year of the "Big Storm," I got a taste of what "a little" can really mean.

My parents, my three younger sisters, and I lived in a spacious two-story house a few hours south of Grandmother Rose. One early summer day, the sky darkened earlier than usual. From our backyard, I saw it swirl into an eerie black-green, and I was struck with an uneasy chill. Still transfixed by the sky, I heard a siren wail and, almost at the same time, my mother calling for me to get in the cellar.

As my mother and we four girls quietly shivered in the dark cellar, a fierce tornado shook the house by the foundation. The wind screamed, and tree limbs fell thundering to the ground. And then, suddenly, there was silence. By the time we surfaced from the basement, the storm had leveled our home and half of our small Indiana town. No one was hurt, but we were homeless.

Tearfully, we girls gathered up what belongings hadn't been destroyed or blown away, stuck them in a cardboard box, and got in our amazingly intact car. We cried all the way to Grandmother Rose's house, where we were to stay while our parents rebuilt the demolished house. They knew that rebuilding wasn't possible with us underfoot.

But, I wondered to myself as we rode past endless cornfields, *how could we possibly all fit into Grandmother Rose's house?*

When we arrived, Grandma ushered each of us to our rooms. The two youngest girls, Rachel and Sandi, shared the sewing room, now divided by an old, white sheet on which Grandmother Rose had drawn pictures of apple trees; a bright, shining sun; and a greeting written in bright red: "Welcome!" Over the next few months, that sheet became a gallery to which we attached drawings, letters from our parents, pictures, and notes.

The ingenuity to turn a little into a lot is a good trait to have while rebuilding—a necessary task that the storms of life often demand.

Jessie moved into the large closet beneath the stairs. Emptied of its usual mismatched items, it comfortably held a cot, peach-crate dressing table, and pictures cut from catalogs to serve as posters on the wall.

For me, Grandmother Rose had converted the enclosed back porch to a private room complete with a mattress on the floor piled with colorful pillows, a stack of books, and a reading lamp. I would sometimes stay up late into the night reading those old, yellowing books. The antique wringer-washer, pushed into the corner and covered with a quilt to double as a table, held Grandma's old wooden radio. If a little was not a lot, it certainly was enough to make us feel at home.

The next few months really tested our creativity. Our big dollhouse at home had been blown to smithereens, but Grandmother Rose helped us make one from shoe boxes, with thread-spool furniture and little people cut from magazines. It was just the right size for carrying outdoors to play with on blankets spread beneath the apple trees. Fragrant white blossoms fluttered down on our miniature neighborhood like snow.

Even though there wasn't any extra money (or time, for Grandma, with an orchard to run) for us to take a vacation, in the languid days of August, Grandmother Rose let the apples hang on the trees for a while, and we "traveled" to the back of the orchard and set up camp. For three days we cooked over a campfire (we even made a Dutch oven apple crisp!), slept on the ground, and listened to the frogs that sang us to sleep.

On rainy days, we played in Grandma's attic. We spent hours dressing up in old clothes and putting on plays. Grandma brought us fresh apple juice to sample and was always a willing audience for our performances.

Then—as sudden as that fateful storm—came the announcement that our house had been repaired. Our parents were on their way. It was time to go home.

"Time to get you out of this cramped place," our mother said apologetically the next day when she came to pick us up. All she saw were makeshift rooms, Grandmother Rose's kitchen overflowing with apples, cider jugs, the cider press, and projects pushed into every corner. It had taken me a whole summer's worth of Grandma's "little into a lot" magic to see past these trivialities, so I didn't try to change my mother's mind on the car trip back home. Instead, my sisters and I insisted on going to Grandmother Rose's the following summer, and all those afterward. We learned how to make all kinds of things out of apples: cider, pies, butter, and even wrinkled apple dolls. We also learned how to run a business. The time eventually came that Grandmother Rose needed our help in tending her orchard and taking care of her customers. And then the business became ours. My sister Jessie and her family live there and run it to this day.

The ingenuity to turn a little into a lot is a good trait to have while rebuilding—a necessary task that the storms of life often demand. Now, as a grandmother myself, I often fall back on that bit of wisdom. On those days when it seems like there just isn't enough to get me through, I like to make an apple pie. The aroma takes me back to Grandmother Rose's house just long enough to hear her say again, "Easy, child. Let's see what we can make from this."

BY MARGARET ANNE HUFFMAN

On those days when it seems like there just isn't enough to get me through, I like to make an apple pie. The aroma takes me back to Grandmother Rose's house.

BUILDING ON FIRE, HEARTS AFLAME

◆ ◆ ◆

◆ ◆ ◆ ◆

Five times each day, at the sound of the tone, I shut the windowless metal antitheft door to our classroom, turned the lock, and began to teach.

◆ ◆ ◆ ◆

THESE WERE UNDOUBTEDLY the worst times the junior high school had ever known. In the lounges and offices, old-timers reminisced about previous administrations not with the usual melancholy, but with a vengeance. An assistant principal said to me, "Get out of here, kid. Working here is like living in California. You can feel the earth trembling. The end is coming. It's only a matter of time until the whole thing just falls into the sea."

I sat at the morning coffee breaks and shuddered in dismay at my colleagues' pain and disappointment. From their perspectives, 20 to 30 years into their careers, 20 to 30 years spent in one place, the disgust and disgrace was too great—perhaps even insurmountable. As for me, two years into a young career, I struggled to maintain an optimistic point of view. I had known no other professional reality. It was, for me, still all about the students. I planned innovative lessons, wore a jacket and tie, and worked as hard as I could.

The hallways of the building were a lost cause; we referred to them as "no-man's land." Shrill screams echoed from stairways. Broken light fixtures dangled in dark passageways. Hooded groups of shadowy figures lurked around corners or unpredictably rushed through the narrow corridors. Shakedowns happened frequently. Fistfights broke out suddenly and ended abruptly, with the combatants scattering into the crowds before security officers could respond. Gang markings and graffiti covered the walls. There were rumors of unreported rapes. Fire alarms rang incessantly—their shrill gongs, however, were dutifully ignored. We had all fallen for that prank too many times.

This was a building under siege.

Five times each day, at the sound of the tone, I shut the windowless metal antitheft door to our classroom, turned the lock, and began to teach. The students were thankful for this simple structure. We read and wrote. We spoke to one another about literature and writing. Most important, perhaps, we listened to each other. We kept writers' notebooks and used these tools to study poetry, science fiction, and personal narrative, and to undertake research projects.

Marie, a recently arrived immigrant from an English-speaking Caribbean island, could not read when school started that year. By late fall she had mastered the alphabet and, with the help of classmates who transcribed her thickly accented dialect, Marie produced a picture book detailing an experience where she was inexplicably transported by an alien to a new planet. At first the new planet seemed cold and harsh. But as her alien guide explained things the planet became more familiar, and she grew to love this place as much as the home planet she had been torn from. Her alien guide was named Jeff, like me.

The level of engagement within the walls of the classroom was wonderful. But life outside the classroom was worse than ever. One morning that winter we arrived to find that our school's yard was closed. Police vehicles blocked the entrances. As teachers and administrators filtered into the building, we learned that a corpse had been discovered by a member of the custodial crew. Early word from the authorities was that the victim had been shot in the back of the head, execution-style. During recess that afternoon, students played ball and jumped double Dutch around the purple stain in the concrete. An uncertain silence settled in the building. There were far fewer fights and no false alarms. The imposed calm lasted a few days.

During this time, my classes were engaged in a family history research project, practicing interviewing techniques. I had been curious about my own family's history and did the assigned interviews myself to use as a model. I conducted a phone interview with my father and learned a number of things about my paternal great-grandparents that I read to the students from my notebook. My great-grandparents did not, as I had originally thought, come to America from Russia together. My great-grandfather arrived in New York City three years before my great-grandmother. He lived in a tenement and established a fish market just three blocks from our school. My great-grandmother arrived at Great-grandpa's tenement apartment unannounced with my grandfather, a child of six or seven, in tow. Cossacks had destroyed the village, the story went, so they had to flee or die there.

After I shared what I'd learned about my family, the students were set to task. Assate arrived a couple days later brimming with excitement. "Listen to what I found out!" she exclaimed. "My great-great-great-grandmother was born on the west coast of Africa. She came to Jamaica on a slave ship. She died when she was 101!" Assate checked off the name and

We read and wrote. We spoke to one another about literature and writing. Most important, perhaps, we listened to each other.

geographic locale of each great-grandparent on the fingers of her left hand while holding her notebook steady with the right. We were all inspired by the girl's enthusiastic detailing of her family's lineage.

Kevin told us, "My mother had some dreams I didn't know about. Her first was to get an education and graduate from college. The second was to help people less fortunate than us. She thinks the less fortunate are just as important as we are."

All week the discoveries were shared in an unusually calm environment. After a relatively peaceful interval, however, the school's tone returned to chaos. The light fixtures that had been repaired in the stairwells were smashed. Where light had regained entry, darkness once again reigned. The fire bells rang with more frequency and volume.

Once the initial interview and research period was completed, we started designing and organizing narratives. The tightness of the community within the classroom increased daily. One March morning we were working on revising our narratives. A pride-filled sharing celebration was in the works. Morale was high. We were buzzing along.

The fire bells sounded, and the students continued working, unfazed. The muffled commotion in the hallway caught my ear. I gingerly turned the lock, opened the windowless door, and was overcome by the sight and smell of a thick, white haze. I shut the door. "Guys," I said, "this one's for real. Let's get out." Calmly and quickly, the students and I filed through the smoky hallway, down the dark stairwell, and out into the brisk, bright winter morning. We joined the rest of the school just as the fire trucks arrived to douse the flames. Recently delivered cases of toilet tissue had been set ablaze, more smoke than fire. No damage. No injuries.

Each of the children who had followed me into that hazy hallway and down the dark stairwell was clutching their own writer's notebook.

I stood alongside one of my colleagues, shivered, and made small talk. The children did the same. As word began to spread that things would be fine, Angelica, a little waif of a thing in a black cardigan, approached me. "Mr. Moss," she said, "I saw this on your desk so I grabbed it for you." She handed me my black-and-white composition notebook, the one that held the interview with my father about my great-grandparents and the ensuing narrative.

"Thanks," I said. Angelica stepped back to join her cadre of friends. I studied the line of shivering, trembling, hopping-to-stay-warm students, and I noticed something I will never forget. Each of the children who had followed me into that hazy hallway and down the dark stairwell was clutching their own writer's notebook. I knew right there, teeth chattering and all, that, yes, there were many difficulties in this position and that, yes, we were losing some painful battles, but we were definitely winning the war.

BY JEFF MOSS

MARKING THE TRAIL

◆ ◆ ◆

*H*OME FROM COLLEGE, I sat in the front pew hold-ing hands with my mom and sister. The choir sang, *"I go before you always, come follow me...."* I took a few deep breaths to quiet my pounding heart and allowed my mind to wander to one of my favorite childhood memories.

I loved that early morning hike with Dad. The smell of Rocky Mountain pine and the chilly air filled me with vigor as I hus-tled behind him on the trail. The warm sun rose to dry the dew from the tall grass covering our path. I had hiked with Dad a dozen times in my 11 years, but I still worried when the trail disappeared.

"Is there a trail, Dad? I can't find it." I ducked under the aspen branch he held back with his large, sturdy frame. "The Scouts and their dads following us will never be able to find us," I said with mixed delight and concern. "If you weren't here, how would I ever find the way?" He gave my shoulder a reassuring squeeze. "We'll mark our trail."

On his instruction, I gathered rocks and stacked them in a pile. Next, we arranged stones to form an arrow pointing uphill. "This shows any-body behind us which way to go," he coached.

Around the next bend, I collected a few more stones and formed them in another small heap. "Now they can follow us easily," I beamed.

◆ ◆ ◆ ◆

Before beginning our trek back, Dad arranged rocks in a circle, then placed a single rock in the center. "This marks the end of the trail," he said. "This will tell those who follow that we went home."

◆ ◆ ◆ ◆

We repeated these rock formations several times as I panted and stumbled over the steep terrain, following Dad's big footprints in the soft dirt.

Feeling more exhilarated than fatigued, we finally reached the summit. There we sat in silence on the rocky peak, listening to nature's concert orchestrated by the wind, birds, and streams. Dad gestured toward an eagle that was soaring in the cobalt sky. Squirrels scampered eagerly to our backpacks, looking for treats, while a doe stepped cautiously onto the clearing, then bolted back into the trees with her fawn close behind.

I knew my dad created these moments especially for me. I was always the youngest Scout and frequently missed out on adventures my older brother and sister experienced. Dad loved his role as an adult leader because it allowed him to combine the three loves of his life: his family, his faith, and the great outdoors.

Storm clouds gathered over a faraway ridge. Thunder rumbled as the distant clouds collided in a clash of lightning.

"Did I ever tell you about how I really found God during the war?" Dad asked, breaking the silence. I knew he enjoyed telling that story almost as much I as enjoyed hearing it over and over again.

I knew it by heart. He had taken a break from maintaining the generators that provided electricity for his platoon. Sitting atop a hill, he watched the earth burning in patches below. When a magnificent lightning storm illuminated the blackened sky, he realized no human-made electricity could compare to that of the Divine Creator. "That's when I knew, and I have never doubted him since," Dad nodded with a smile.

I reached for his hand and held it tight as we watched the power sparks in the distance.

When he said it was time to leave, I groaned in protest. I didn't want this treasured moment to end. He reminded me that, while we loved the trail, there are often better things at the end. "Like Mom and her pancakes waiting back at camp!"

Before beginning our trek back, Dad arranged rocks in a circle, then placed a single rock in the center. "This marks the end of the trail," he said. "This will tell those who follow that we went home."

Several years later, Dad was diagnosed with ALS, amyotrophic lateral sclerosis, otherwise known as Lou Gehrig's disease. His most difficult path of life lay ahead. We learned all we could about the incurable, debilitating illness while Dad's ability to eat and speak gradually diminished. Accepting his impending death with courage and faith, he continued to show me the way.

He led me through earning my Eagle Scout award. I followed in his footsteps when I was confirmed in my faith. He guided me through the rocky path of high school graduation and choosing a college. He brought me and my mom, grandma, aunt, and uncle together to pray after church every Sunday. In written notes, he told us that while he loved life's journey, he looked forward to eternity with the Master Electrician.

My sister tugged gently on my hand. The choir ended the refrain, and the piano played softly as Father Bob offered the final funeral prayer. Dozens of Scouts and former Scouts came forward, placing a circle of rocks on the altar. Together my sister, brother, and I placed the single rock in the center.

It was the end of the trail. Dad had gone home.

BY LeANN THIEMAN, FOR TIM CHANEY

ANGELS ALL AROUND

◈ ◈ ◈ ◈

*A*ND WHEN *we come to think of it, goodness is uneventful. It does not flash, it glows. It is deep, quiet, and very simple. It passes not with oratory, it is commonly foreign to riches, nor does it often sit in the places of the mighty: but may be felt in the touch of a friendly hand or the look of a kindly eye.*

—DAVID GRAYSON

THE KINDNESS OF STRANGERS

❖ ❖ ❖

The stranger who's a neighbor becomes an angel through their kindness.

HERE'S A FAMOUS LINE in the classic play *A Streetcar Named Desire* that says, "I have always depended on the kindness of strangers." This has certainly been true for me.

The Bible speaks of "attending angels unaware" and guardian angels, but I have learned that "angels" are not always immortal beings from heaven. Because they are God's messengers, they can come in many forms. The dictionary says an angel can also be "a kind and lovable person." These are the kinds of angels I've encountered often in my lifetime.

One time someone ran into my mailbox during the night. When I called the post office in the morning, I was told to also report it to the State Police. After the officer looked over the damage and wrote up a report, he mentioned that he would be off the next day and would stop by to "fix it up." I thought he meant to put in some nails to hold the splintered wood together. But he arrived with a thick post, post-hole digger, and cement for the base support. When the officer was finished, all he would accept for his generosity and hard work was a cup of coffee.

People have joked with me that my car is a nail magnet. I get two or three new tires every year. In fact, I've lost track of how many times a stranger has stopped to help me fix a flat tire, only to smile and wave away any notion of reward other than my genuine words of thanks.

Then there was the summer my lawnmower was broken. I came home from work to find my nearly one-acre lawn newly mown on more than one occasion until my mower was fixed. One winter it snowed for days and drifted too deep for me to get the car out of the yard. I heard a loud motor sound outside and ran to the door to see a plow clearing my driveway. On its second pass the driver smiled, waved, and kept on going. The smile and wave seem to be trademarks of kind strangers. There are times when I've come home to find a dazzling basket of fresh vegetables sitting on my back step. There's never a note.

I live in the country, where we call each other "neighbors" even if we live ten miles apart and don't know each other's name. Sometimes we recognize a face or passing car without really knowing the person. But in a time of need, the stranger who's a neighbor becomes an angel through their kindness.

My most dramatic encounter happened on a cold, drizzly winter night. On my way to work in the morning I noticed that the dashboard reading for my car's battery volts was low. Since the battery was fairly new, I thought it might be a computer misread. I figured I would stop to get it checked on my way home that night.

That evening, riding on a busy three-lane highway, I noticed the car was steadily losing power but surged if nothing was running. I immediately turned off the lights, wipers, radio, and heater, and rode down the shoulder with the flashers on. It was risky, but I only had another mile to go to get to the auto repair shop. I prayed the whole way, "Please just let me make it off the exit ramp and to the shop." As I coasted through the toll booth, the car died.

Frustrated, I didn't know what to do. Just then a knock on my window startled me. It was the driver of the vehicle behind me. Amazingly, in this day of road rage, he had never honked or yelled. Instead, he was offering to push my car with his pickup and help me. Once we steered out of the way, he popped the hood and checked it out. I was explaining to him how the car had acted, and he said it must have been the alternator that failed and I had drained the battery of whatever stored charge it had left. He offered me a ride to the auto shop. When we got there, he told the circumstances to the mechanic and requested a loaner battery to get the car to the shop without being towed.

Once we got back to my car it took another 45 minutes to rig the other battery up. Unfortunately, neither one of us had the appropriate tools for making the job easier. Somehow, despite the steady, icy drizzle and aggravating circumstances, the man never visibly or verbally lost his temper.

When he finally got my car to run, he followed me back to the shop and squared things with the mechanic. Then he offered to drive me home. By now he had spent an hour and a half of his time with me and was soaked to the skin. His supper was probably drying out or cold by now. Even if I only lived five blocks away, I couldn't bring myself to let him do any more—I felt bad enough already. I didn't even have five dollars to offer him. I knew I could call someone to come get me, so I told him to go home and change his clothes.

I believe that for every act of kindness, every smile we send out, another will return to us.

I asked him if he was married and he was. I patted him on the shoulder and said, "Tell your wife not to be angry with you for being late. Tell her she's married to an angel because tonight you have been my guardian angel. God sent you to look out for me." Later, I thought I should at least send him a thank you card, but I realized I hadn't found out his name, where he lived, or where he worked.

Sometimes we hear people speak of "what goes around comes around." They often say it in a negative way, referring to someone who's mean or done something spiteful, implying they will "get theirs" someday. However, for every negative there's a positive. I believe that for every act of kindness, every smile we send out, another will return to us. Kindness has that sort of boomerang effect.

All the people I've mentioned—and the many I didn't have room to include—are the true epitome of angels. They offer their kindness without any thought of reward. They do good deeds because for them it seems like the right thing to do. For all my angels, I pray God will bless them a thousand times in return just as he has blessed me by sending them into my life. I've depended on their kindness, and they have never let me down.

BY DEBY MURRAY

WHEN I STUMBLED...

◇ ◇ ◇

"OH, WHAT a beautiful, glorious day!" That's what I wanted to shout as my young son and I hurried out the front door one busy fall morning.

I glanced at my watch: 8:00. I had plenty of time for an invigorating walk to work in the fresh autumn air. Although it was already late November, the sky was bright and cloudless. All the better to show off the brand-new magenta jumper I had just bought for work. Yes, I know that magenta is a rather bright color for work. But I'm a preschool teacher, and "bright" is exactly what my students love—the wilder the color, the better!

I guess I've always loved teaching. Especially little ones. I love to read stories to them, introduce them to the alphabet and numbers, sing with them, see the world through their eyes. In fact, I get as excited about new projects as they do.

So, of course, I hate to miss a single day of work. Besides, little ones need the security of being around the same adults each day, as much as possible. It's as hard on them when a teacher is out sick as it is on the teacher!

That's why I felt so discouraged earlier this fall when I seemed to be developing some health problems. I had even fainted one day in October. Grim memories of childhood illnesses haunted me. I always felt so ashamed when I was sick—as though it was all my fault. So I'd been

checking in regularly with my doctor. Things seemed to be under control now, and that was just fine with me. I needed all the energy and creativity I could muster to keep up with a roomful of wiggly, giggly, four-year-olds. And then I also had my own lively son at home! I also needed plenty of energy to get ready for Thanksgiving, which was coming up quickly. I knew the added stress could take its toll.

Those arms had been so comforting, so blessing, so warm…as comforting and blessing as those of an angel.

I suddenly felt a little lightheaded, just as I had for a few moments while getting dressed earlier that morning. But I took a deep breath, and the feeling passed. *Please, dear God, let me be all right today.*

Out on the sidewalk, my son, Daniel, and I turned back to wave to our new home. How I loved living here! We luxuriated in being able to spread out in a roomy house after years in a cramped apartment. Best of all, we now lived close enough for both Daniel and I to walk to our schools.

The last couple years he had gone to preschool with me. But now, as a very "grown-up" kindergartner, Daniel attended an elementary school just a couple blocks away, which worked out perfectly. Neighborhood kids were his school pals, a friend of mine from church watched him after class, and my mom had been the school's office manager for years. Everyone knew my mom, and Daniel was thrilled to be able to see her every day.

The nearby preschool where I taught was located in the church I had attended most of my life. It was also where Jay and I were married. This special place was where I first learned about God's protection and care of those who love him. How he sent an angel to protect Daniel in the lions' den and another one to rescue Peter from prison. Why, perhaps this very moment there were angels surrounding Daniel and me to keep us safe as we set off to school!

"There's your school, Daniel!" I said as we rounded the corner. The streets and sidewalks around us were jammed as usual, with parents dropping off carload after carload of excited children. "Good-bye! Have a great day. Say hi to Grandma for me. And think about what you'd like to eat for Thanksgiving!"

As Daniel rushed off to meet his classmates, I shifted the weight of my bags and headed for my own school. High overhead I could see some migrating geese. The yards around me were bright with mums, as well as gold and crimson leaves. The laughter of children filled the air.

As the morning traffic whizzed past me, I began planning for my own school day ahead. The children always loved making handprint "turkeys," so that would be one of our fun projects. We were also going to make Pilgrim hats for our classroom's Thanksgiving celebration later in the week. And thanks to some of our parent volunteers, we were planning to have a complete Thanksgiving dinner at school.

Why, perhaps this very moment there were angels surrounding Daniel and me to keep us safe as we set off to school!

Then, of course, there were my own holiday plans to make. This year, to celebrate our first Thanksgiving in our new home, we had invited a houseful of friends, relatives, and coworkers.

I was thrilled, of course. But apprehensive as well. My mother and mother-in-law would both help cook. But this was my first time hosting a big family holiday. There were all those exhausting details to take care of, like finding enough silverware and plates—plus places for everyone to sit without falling on top of each other. And, of course, I'd have to clean the entire house from top to bottom!

Indeed, just before my husband Jay kissed me and left for his own job that morning, I reminded him that we needed to run to the supermarket that evening to get our turkey. I'd finally saved up enough register receipts to get one for free! Already my mind was running through a shopping list of other absolute necessities: pies, yams, gravy, string beans, corn. Plus, of course, cranberries, salad, dressing—the whole works!

With my head full of plans, I stepped off the curb to cross the street. The next thing I knew, I was sprawled in the middle of the street, barely able to lift my head off the ground.

What in the world had happened? Obviously I'd had a very bad fall. But, why? Did I slip on something? Step off the curb wrong? Turn my ankle? *Or had I fainted again?*

As soon as I could sit up, I checked myself for damage. The contents of my purse, schoolbag, and lunchbox were scattered everywhere. But, amazingly, I had suffered no cuts, no broken bones, no bruises, no swollen ankles. Indeed, no pain of any kind. Just a black stain on one shoulder of my new jumper and a huge hole in my pantyhose.

Suddenly I remembered that I was sitting right in the middle of a very busy street. Terrified, I looked around for oncoming cars. But, amazingly, the street—which had been so crowded just moments before—was now completely empty. It was as though I were out in the middle of a vast desert.

Or a sanctuary. And then I realized something else. I wasn't alone. A strange woman was right there—to one side and sort of behind me—holding me tight.

Because I was still confused, and my hair had fallen down over my face, I couldn't see the woman very well. But I did notice that her hair was dark like mine. And she seemed to be dressed in gleaming white.

"Are you all right, honey?" she asked, her voice full of gentle concern.

"Y-yes. Uh, of course, I'm fine."

I was so embarrassed! What if she were the mother of one of my students? Or even one of the new teachers at Daniel's school! If so, she'd probably tell my mom all about it, and I'd never hear the end of it. Mom had always been protective of me, and she had been really worried about my health this fall. In fact, she'd been insisting that I let her drive me to school each morning. I was the one who kept protesting, "But walking's so healthy!"

"Now you're sure?" the woman in white repeated.

I nodded. "Yes, but thanks again. I really appreciate your help."

Forcing a laugh, I pulled away and started snatching up all my scattered belongings. If this woman had seen me fall, maybe other people had, too. Tumbles really aren't dignified for a schoolteacher, and I certainly didn't want to set anyone's tongue wagging.

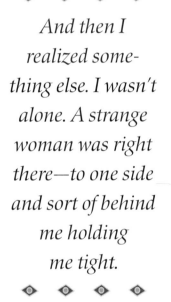

And then I realized something else. I wasn't alone. A strange woman was right there—to one side and sort of behind me holding me tight.

Collecting my bags, I insisted, "I'll be just fine, honest." As the woman helped me get up, I reached out to shake my good Samaritan's hand and say good-bye.

But there was no one there.

In fact, there was no one but me in the street, on the sidewalk, in the general vicinity.

Everything was as quiet as if someone had turned off all the sound— as if even time itself had stopped. Or as if God had built an invisible, soundproof wall all around me. Then, just like that, all the noises rushed back. Parents, children, and cars whizzed by again. I brushed myself off, reorganized my belongings, and straightened up my clothes. Then I walked on to school and my normal workday world, just as if nothing had happened.

But, of course, something *had* happened. I had a big stain on my shoulder and torn pantyhose to remind me of that. Along with the still-felt touch of those strong but gentle arms. Whoever's arms they were.

To this day, I still don't know if my mysterious comforter that morning was just another woman who happened to be passing by—a neighbor, a mother who had already delivered her child to school, or one of the school staff.

Or if she was a special divine being God had sent to help me, just as I had asked him to, by protecting me from injuring myself in that fall. And from being hit by a speeding car. Just as he long ago sent his angels to protect Daniel and Peter.

Those arms had been so comforting, so blessing, so warm… as comforting and blessing as those of an angel. So full of God's love,

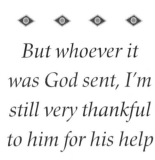

But whoever it was God sent, I'm still very thankful to him for his help both right then and in the busy days that followed.

strength, and compassion. I do know that his Word promises, "He will command his angels concerning you to guard you in all your ways; they will lift you up in their hands" (Psalm 91:11–12, NIV). And I believe that promise with all my heart.

Amazingly, although every accident near the school was normally reported to the school office, no one ever reported mine. Nobody told my mom or called me up at work or home afterward to check on me.

Maybe I'll never know the identity of my rescuer. But whoever it was God sent, I'm still very thankful to him for his help both right then and in the busy days that followed. Not that our holiday turned out absolutely perfect: My husband got the flu, the turkey was hard to carve, and the yams were scorched. But even so, everyone who came said it was their best Thanksgiving ever. I know it was for me. I'm *still* giving thanks!

BY VIKKI DENISI HANSON,
AS TOLD TO BONNIE COMPTON HANSON

ROADSIDE RESCUE

◈ ◈ ◈

*A*T'S A GOOD THING the summer wedding was beautiful, because the rest of the day held nothing but problems. My friend John and I had borrowed my dad's car to attend the wedding of a college friend 150 miles away. Shortly after our venture began, John discovered he had forgotten his wallet at home. Then, on the way back, John got really sick.

That's when the car died at the side of the interstate.

Over and over, I turned the key, pumped the accelerator, and rocked with the sound of the groaning engine.

"Where's my guardian angel when I need her?" I moaned.

"It's 7:00," John said, squinting at his watch. "We'd better walk back to that gas station before it closes."

I led my nauseated friend down the shoulder of the highway. It was hard to tell if he was sweating from the 96-degree heat or from his fever. My white high heels clicked on the pavement, and the strand of imitation pearls clung to my sweaty neck.

I called Dad from the gas station and listened to his mechanical advice. If his suggestions didn't work, I'd have to call a tow truck.

"It's 7:15," Mom said into the speakerphone. "If you aren't back on the road in one hour, call again so we know how you're doing." She tried not to worry about me now that I was in college, but at times like these I knew she couldn't help it.

John and I plodded back down the scorching pavement to the car and tried Dad's long-distance advice. The car coughed and choked but refused to start.

I leaned against the steering wheel. "What if no one stops to help us?"

"What if someone does?" John worried out loud. He propped his aching head on the dashboard while we swapped tales of horrible crimes that happened along the highway.

At 7:50, we admitted our defeat and walked across the highway to head back to the gas station. Just then, a dilapidated station wagon sputtered to a stop in front of our car. I could see the two male occupants through the missing rear window. The driver's long, stringy hair touched the shoulders of his ragged shirt. As we stood across the road from them, John and I agreed they looked pretty rough.

"And we look pretty rich," John said, motioning to our wedding attire. "Think they'll believe we're poor college students?"

"Need some help?" the driver hollered. His smile leered through his scraggly beard. As we headed back across the interstate, we could see that the sleeves had been torn from the denim jacket the man was wearing. His tall leather moccasins had fringe hanging just beneath the knees of his torn blue jeans.

"I always knew my guardian angel would be unique," I teased in a whisper. "Maybe he'll help us."

"Or rob us," John cautioned as we neared our car.

A second man exited the station wagon. I thanked them both for stopping and, with trembling hands, released the hood, hoping I wasn't making a big mistake by letting them help us.

"I always knew my guardian angel would be unique," I teased in a whisper.

The driver bent over the car engine. I read the back of his worn jacket: Christian Motorcycle Association. John and I beamed at each other. I nodded and winked—and breathed a sigh of relief.

Within minutes, the car was running and the four of us stood together smiling and shaking hands. John and I offered them the only money we had with us: five dollars each, some of it in change. They accepted it gratefully, saying it was more than they'd had in a long time.

I drove home, collapsed in the chair, and recounted my "guardian angel" story to my parents.

Mom's face was serious. "What time did they stop?"

I thought for a minute. "About ten minutes to 8:00."

She smiled at Dad. "I looked at my watch at 7:50 and said to Dad, 'Let's pray an angel stops to help her.'"

Dad said, "That's when I sent you mine."

BY LeAnn Thieman, for Christie Thieman

MY CHRISTMAS ANGEL FRIEND

◆ ◆ ◆

This is what Christmas is really about, I thought. *God gave his best to us—his only son —and now a new friend is giving her best to me.*

"MARY IS SO CONCERNED about you, it's starting to affect her schoolwork," my daughter's fourth-grade teacher solemnly told me during a parent-teacher conference. "She's really worried about you." With a sense of guilt and shame, I realized that my personal problems were having a damaging effect on my youngest child, Mary.

I was embarrassed that the teacher had learned about my personal difficulties through my daughter. I mumbled apologetically that my 70-year-old mother had died suddenly only weeks before from a stroke. I explained that although I had been depressed over her death, I never dreamed that nine-year-old Mary had been so perceptive of my pain.

Quickly thinking back, I remembered the breakfast in bed that Mary had served me the week before. Bringing dry toast and canned juice to me was her way of trying to lift my spirits. But I had been too depressed to realize her deep concern, even though I'd been touched by getting breakfast in bed—a luxury I'd never received before, not even on Mother's Day.

Now it was only three weeks before Christmas, and I couldn't get into the spirit of the season. I hadn't baked any cookies or started my shopping. Could it be because Thanksgiving had been such a disaster, and I feared that Christmas might be even worse?

With a heavy heart, I had prepared and served the traditional Thanksgiving dinner for my husband, our four children, and my widowed father. We all felt something was missing—my mother. I tried to be cheerful, especially to help my elderly father get through the day. I held up fairly well until it was time to wash the dishes and put them away. Then I started crying because the after-dinner clean-up had always been a special time for Mother and me. We would talk and share many things as we worked side by side in the kitchen.

Now Mother was gone, and I felt as if I couldn't carry on the coming Christmas celebration without her. I needed her! My husband and children tried to help me get into the spirit of the season, but I secretly wished we could skip Christmas this year. I just didn't have the energy for it.

My husband put up a beautiful lighted nativity scene outdoors. The children helped decorate the house, and everything looked lovely, but I still could not overcome my deep sense of loss. Mother had always been an essential part of our Christmas festivities, and now she wasn't around to share in the preparations. During this holiday season, I wanted her advice and assistance on everything from making and wrapping gifts for the children to baking traditional treats like Bohemian kolackys, a fruit-filled pastry my family loves.

My husband insisted that he take me shopping to select a new Christmas outfit. He thought new clothes might cheer me up. I protested that I didn't need anything. "I have several really nice dresses," I told him. But he persisted. "Wouldn't you like to have something new to wear to Christmas parties?" I told him emphatically that I did not want to go to any Christmas parties. I explained that I preferred to be left alone in my grief.

Finally, I consented to go shopping with him. After looking numbly through racks of clothes, I chose a matching three-piece white linen outfit. I brought the outfit home and hung it in the closet, still not feeling any joy—only guilt for not being excited about my new clothes.

At a church potluck one night, I confided to another woman that I was having trouble getting into the spirit of Christmas this year since my mother had passed away only a few weeks earlier. "It's so hard. I just can't find any joy in the season," I told her sadly, admitting my wish to forgo Christmas entirely.

After listening sympathetically, the woman tried to console me, and she encouraged me to get into the holiday spirit for the sake of my family. But even her kind words didn't help.

As Christmas drew nearer, I became even more depressed. I forced myself to buy and wrap some gifts for my husband, my father, and my children. I can't even remember now what I bought, but I know I didn't put much thought or love into the gifts. I did bake a few simple sugar cookies, but I didn't decorate them, and I couldn't bring myself to make the usual fancy holiday goodies. "These cookies will just have to do," I sighed.

Two days before Christmas, the lady who had so lovingly listened to my troubles at the church dinner called me at home. She told me that she had made an extra dish of the Mexican casserole I had liked so much at the church potluck, and she asked if she could bring it over to me while it was still hot.

◆ ◆ ◆ ◆

The radiant warmth of the manger scene made my heart swell, and a lump formed in my throat.

◆ ◆ ◆ ◆

As I waited for her to arrive, I decided to step outside into the cool night air. Shivering and alone, I stared at the dark nativity scene, with the wind blowing through me. Then I turned on the lights.

The radiant warmth of the manger scene made my heart swell, and a lump formed in my throat. *This is what Christmas is really about,* I thought. *God gave his best to us—his only son—and now a new friend is giving her best to me.*

When the woman arrived, I greeted her cheerfully. We stood in front of the lighted Bethlehem scene, reflecting on the age-old story of the first Christmas. Awkwardly, she held the hot casserole out as her "offering" to me as a friend and fellow Christian.

"I wanted to give you something…because…you're just you," she stammered, slightly embarrassed, not knowing how to explain her unexpected gift from the heart. I smiled and thanked her, thinking what a beautiful compliment she had just given me.

I looked back at the nativity scene and gave thanks to God for my Christmas angel friend. With her heartfelt gifts of food and friendship, she seemed to me like an angel coming to proclaim the Good News of Christmas. Her generous, caring holiday spirit pushed away the depression I had been fighting for weeks and ushered in the true loving spirit of the season. Thanks to my new friend, I was able to celebrate the birthday of Jesus with joy and peace in my heart.

BY MARGARET MALSAM

THE VOICE OF AN ANGEL: DELLA REESE

◈　◈　◈

*M*OST PEOPLE KNOW Della Reese as wise, motherly Tess on the hit show *Touched by an Angel*. But long before portraying an angel on television, Della felt the presence of angelic beings in her own life. Her unwavering faith in God and trust in his plan for her life have carried Della through heartwrenching lows and exhilarating highs, bringing her to the wonderful place she's at today.

IN THE PRESENCE OF ANGELS

One evening near the end of the 1960s, successful gospel singer Della Reese and her nine-year-old daughter, Deloreese, were splashing around in their swimming pool. Unaware that Dumpsey (her daughter's nickname) had shut the open door when she joined her mom outside, Della stepped from the pool and smashed through the glass patio door.

Pinned between jagged slices of glass, Della tried to free herself, but every direction she moved caused slivers of glass to cut into her body. "[I was] unaware that the top piece of the glass was seconds away from falling straight down and decapitating me," Della wrote in her 1997 autobiography *Angels Along the Way: My Life with Help from Above*. "My mother [Nellie] who had died in 1949…reached around from behind me, taking hold of my head and shoulders, and lifted me up onto my feet."

Dumpsey witnessed the accident and raced to a neighbor's house for help. Soon, doctors and paramedics worked feverishly to save Della's life, unaware that an angel had already intervened. "I smelled her," Della recalls, describing the vanilla and spices her mom, a cook, always trailed in her wake. "It was my mama." Nellie's spirit never left Della's side as 1,000 stitches repaired her cuts and seven pints of blood were returned to her veins.

Since that day, Della has often been asked if she and God became closer as a result of this incident. Her answer might surprise you. "It didn't make me any closer to God," Della insists, since he was already a major part of her life. To prove her point, Della recalls another miracle that happened ten years after her close encounter with the patio door.

Rehearsing for an appearance on NBC television's the *Tonight Show* in 1979, Della practiced her songs with the band until she "hit the flattest note I've ever sung." Seconds later, she slumped to the floor. "As I fell, I put myself in God's hands," she later wrote. Rushed to Burbank's St. Joseph Hospital, Della was diagnosed with a brain aneurysm, a usually fatal defect closely tied to the trauma that had killed her mother three decades before.

Given little chance of living through the night, Della lay unconscious as doctors delivered devastating news to her companion (now husband), Franklin Lett. If Della *did* survive, they told him, she'd likely be blind, crippled, or worse. Franklin sat beside her and prayed all night.

His prayers, and those of everyone else in Della's life, sustained her. To everyone's relief and delight, she awoke at dawn. Tests revealed other weaknesses in her brain, so as quickly as she could be stabilized and moved, Della was flown to London University Hospital in Ontario, Canada, for two delicate operations.

With therapy and the support of her personal legion of "angels," Reese bounced back with the optimism that shines through her public persona and pervades her personal life as well. Having God "hold on to her," just like her mother had done when Della walked through that glass door, is a recurrent theme that reaches all the way back to her childhood.

IN THE BEGINNING . . .

Observing such wonders on a regular basis convinced young Della to put her faith where her mom always placed it: in the Lord.

Born Deloreese Patricia Early in 1931 to Richard and Nellie Early, the now-famous singer, actress, minister, and television angel knew plenty of poverty despite the best efforts of her hardworking parents. Happily, material goods weren't the focus of the Early household—God was. Della's most beloved childhood recollections include instances that show her mother's personal relationship with God. One time Nellie remarked aloud, as though she just wanted the Lord to know, that there was no bread in the house. Soon after, a neighbor with an extra loaf appeared at the front door. Observing such wonders on a regular basis convinced young Della to put her faith where her mom always placed it: in the Lord.

Della's prayerful outlook was not limited to life-threatening situations. She sought God's counsel about her career, too—a natural move since Della had sung at the neighborhood church from the time she was six years old. It hadn't taken long for the girl's remarkable voice to attract the attention of choir members and congregants alike. She became a featured singer on Sundays and started performing outside the church as well. "I was very small, but I could carry a tune and remember the words," she wrote in her autobiography. Della even toured the country as a backup singer for gospel great Mahalia Jackson when she was only 13.

Though her beloved mom died of a cerebral hemorrhage when Della was just 17, she kept going, knowing her mother's spirit would always be with her. In less than a decade, Della received her first recording contract, celebrated her first hit record (*And that Reminds Me*), and adopted a beautiful daughter. Through two troubled marriages, Della kept her self-esteem and her faith in God intact. When she eventually asked the Lord to choose a husband for her, Franklin Lett came into her life, and the couple married in 1979. Her personal and professional blessings have continually multiplied. God's light pointed her footsteps down a path of success, and Della followed without hesitation.

FROM TV TALK SHOW HOST TO TALKS WITH GOD

Today's television talk shows barely resemble those of the 1960s and '70s, so Reese was able to host *Della*, her own variety show—the first ever hosted by a black woman—without compromising her beliefs (the show aired in 1969 and 1970). But ever since the accident involving the glass door, Della's career had begun to take a backseat to introspection. What did God have in mind for her after saving her from death? She prayed for answers, asking God to send a minister to her. Once more, Della received an unlikely response: God instructed Della to become a minister.

Not one to question so lofty an order, Della enrolled in an eight-year-long program at Chicago's Johnnie Coleman Institute. Ordained as a minister in 1987, Della built a huge congregational base from her California home, moving to larger quarters as her flock increased. Yet even more miracles were in store for her. In 1993, Della was offered a starring role in

Touched by an Angel. These days, she flies back and forth between her 350-member Understanding Principles for Better Living Church congregation in Los Angeles and the Utah set of her popular TV show.

Premiered with little fanfare, *Touched by an Angel* was initially a ratings disaster, but Della assured the cast and crew that the Lord had his own plans for them. Sure enough, by its second year, the series skyrocketed into the top ten. Della plays Tess, a wise, no-nonsense angel who spends her days mentoring new angel Monica, played by Roma Downey. Each week, viewers watch them travel from place to place, helping men and women see the kindness, love, and compassion in others. Costar Downey told the *Atlanta Journal-Constitution,* "We get so much fan mail each week that Della and I sit in our trailers together, reading them and crying." Rarely a day goes by that fans don't say "your show changed our lives."

ADDING HER SPECIAL TOUCH OF LOVE

According to *Touched by an Angel* staffers, Della is a "serial hugger" and smoocher who dispenses hugs before filming begins each day, and she's always on hand to help with out-of-the-ordinary problems arising on the set. For example, early in the show, when ratings were low and a spot on the next year's lineup was tenuous, Della told her costars, "This is a God thing and it's going to be fine. No matter how funky it looks, just hang on." They did. You know the rest.

On another occasion, the temperature at their Utah shoot site reached an unbearable 109 degrees. Walking into the hot sun, Reese lifted her arms and proclaimed, "Lord, we need a cloud, and we need it now." Within minutes, big billowing tufts rolled in. The temperature dropped 10 degrees. So did jaws. Filming resumed.

◆ ◆ ◆ ◆

"God's work is like dropping a pebble in the water," Della explains. "The ripples go on forever.

◆ ◆ ◆ ◆

"God's work is like dropping a pebble in the water," Della explains. "The ripples go on forever. Have you ever noticed? God will give you something that will help somebody that'll help somebody else. Then that will turn around, come back, and help you."

Given so resolute a spirit, Della Reese's warmth, conviction, and depth of love for God cannot help but dazzle everyone with whom she comes in contact. But perhaps the full and complete meaning of so blessed a life can be summed up in Della's own words, taken from her autobiography, in which she charges each of us to do God's work: "I believe if each of you would look back over your life, you would see God's hand in it—in His hand, your hand—or you would have never made it this far. Be of good courage and do what you want to do. Relax in the reality and joy that you are empowered with the spirit of God. Just as there have been angels along the way to watch over me, there are angels watching over you right this second."

BY GAIL COHEN

MY SPECIAL ANGEL

◆ ◆ ◆

As I walked closer to the kitten, our eyes met. There was an instant attraction, and I knew in my heart she was meant for me.

◆ ◆ ◆ ◆

MY HUSBAND, Jim, and I have always been blessed with a house full of cats. We've shared our home with 11 feline friends over the years, all of whom were strays or from an animal shelter. We also run an "outdoor cafe" on our porch to feed countless other strays.

Weenie, our oldest and dearest cat, died in the fall of 1996. This was an especially painful time for us because I had recently suffered the loss of my entire family. Over a period of 11 months, my mother, father, and brother had all died of cancer. I was becoming increasingly depressed and could not bear the thought of the normally joyous holiday season without my family.

My downward slide became apparent at work, especially to a dear young man named Patrick. He and I had formed a close bond immediately after I started my job. His great sense of humor and love of laughter and practical jokes had instantly drawn me to him—he reminded me a great deal of my brother.

I was also one of the few people who could see through the comedian Patrick was on the outside to find the hurting teenager on the inside, who was crying out for attention and understanding. He and I were both from broken homes and had an overwhelming need to be loved. Perhaps that is what had really drawn me to him—in many ways, I could understand his pain. And, as I found out, he could understand mine.

It disturbed Patrick to see me so depressed, especially at Christmastime. Knowing of my great affection for cats and how much the recent loss of Weenie had added to my depression, Patrick decided to take action.

He had heard about a poor little kitten that had been left to die, but, miraculously, someone had heard her faint cries and rescued her. She was taken to a local veterinary clinic, where she was first fed through an eyedropper and then eventually raised on a baby bottle. She spent the first three months of her life in the clinic, receiving constant love and attention from the staff. But Patrick knew he'd found the perfect "mama" for this special kitten.

On December 23, he called me into the kitchen at work and gave me a handsomely wrapped package. Immediately being suspicious of a prank, I shook it. The familiar sound of a box of cat food rattled through the kitchen. Everyone who had gathered there started laughing, so I went along with Patrick's joke. I ripped off the paper and was holding a box of Kitten Chow. By this time, I was laughing, too, and I thanked him. "Well, at least it's something I can always use!" At that moment, he took me by the hand and led me around the corner. There stood another coworker holding the most adorable little kitten I had ever seen! I was so shocked and surprised. I could not believe how kind and thoughtful my young friend had been. There aren't many people who would go to such lengths to give such a meaningful gift.

Patrick looked at me and said, "I figured this was the one thing you needed to cheer you up and help you make it through this Christmas. Having a new kitten to care for will occupy your mind and bring you the happiness you deserve!" I was laughing and crying and hugging him at the same time. For once in my life, I was speechless!

As I walked closer to the kitten, our eyes met. There was an instant attraction, and I knew in my heart she was meant for me. She scrambled into my arms, and crawled up the front of my Christmas Cat sweatshirt until her little head was resting on my right shoulder. It was there that she stayed for the rest of the afternoon, purring contentedly. Others tried to take her from me, but she held on to me for dear life. She had adopted me. I named her Angel, and everyone agreed it was the perfect name for this tiny gift from God—and, of course, from Patrick.

I took Angel home and introduced her to her new brothers and sisters and my stunned but pleased husband. There was no period of adjustment as there had been with the other cats. Angel walked around like she owned the place. It seemed so familiar to her, as if she had been there before. It was then that I realized God had shown her the way, and she had accepted her assignment.

Her first night at home, Angel wasn't satisfied to sleep in the cozy little bed we had carefully prepared for her downstairs. Instead, she followed me up the steps and took her place on my pillow. And she did the same thing every night afterward! She placed her paws around my head as if holding me safely and protecting me from the world. I began to sleep more soundly and peacefully than I had in a very long time.

As Angel grew, we needed to change the sleeping arrangements because I no longer had enough space on my pillow for me! Now she

Angel walked around like she owned the place. It seemed so familiar to her, as if she had been there before.

sleeps right next to me, lengthwise with her head on the pillow nestled close to mine. This gives her close access to my face when she feels the need for hugs and kisses during the night. If I make the "mistake" of trying to roll over and face away from her, she is forced to get up and properly throw herself down again on the other side, letting me know of her displeasure at being disturbed!

Angel always seems to sense when I am having a bad day because she makes it a point to stay as close to me as possible and smother me with extra kisses. She, my husband, and God give me the strength and courage I need to go on another day.

Patrick is always anxious to hear of Angel's latest escapades and mischievous behavior. She makes us both laugh, even more than we did before, and that is quite an accomplishment!

Because of God's love for me and the special friendship I have with Patrick, as well as the unconditional love and understanding from my husband, I have been able to recover from my tremendous losses and enjoy life once again. I firmly believe that God sent me the best gift of all that Christmas, and he used Patrick as the deliveryman.

BY BARBARA SPOTTS

THE ANGEL ON THE BRIDGE

◈ ◈ ◈

*A*M ALIVE today because of an angel, for if an angel had not saved my father, I would never have been born. Of course, this is actually my father's story, and in fact, I never even realized that it was the tale of a guardian angel until my father pointed it out to me just recently.

To be sure, this was always my favorite family story growing up, one I never got tired of hearing over and over at holiday gatherings. Most of Dad's stories were funny—like the time he, as a young schoolboy, forgot he had a slice of custard pie in his coat pocket and sat against it on the school bus—but this particular vignette had an eerie, uncanny quality that stayed with me over the years. How appropriate and ironic then, that when I sent Dad a copy of a magazine about true-life angels, he said that the stories reminded him of his own experience—a connection I myself had never made!

I suppose I should have known all along that my father believed in angels. I was raised Catholic, and at a certain point very early in my childhood, my mother told me to pray that Dad would start going to church regularly with us. I prayed, and he came to church. Yet all along it had been my father who really had the faith, simple and strong.

The angel incident, which happened in 1932 when Dad was three or four years old, started with the neighbor's new car. Or perhaps it really started with the tailor who made Dad a beautiful new sailor coat. It was navy blue with brass buttons and a sturdy belt sewn across the back.

One Sunday afternoon, the neighbors wanted to take my father's family for a drive in their new '33 Ford. My grandmother opted not to go, and she was hesitant about letting young Alfred go off that day. However, as often happened, my strong-willed great-grandmother prevailed.

So my great-grandmother, whom we called "Nonny," and her other daughter, my great-aunt "Tanta," piled into the crowded car with the neighbor family. The husband and wife were in front, with Nonny, Tanta, and my father in the backseat. The car had a soft roof and no window glass. Grandma stayed behind. Everyone thought she was just a worrywart.

It was a beautiful day for a ride and, then as now, the water on a sunny day exerted a magnetic attraction. The driver steered the car through the beautiful Connecticut countryside, from Bridgeport up to Waterbury along the Naugatuck River. The car was filled with the sound of talking and laughing, while little Alfie watched the scenery roll by.

As they headed for home in the late afternoon, it suddenly began to rain. The afternoon travelers were fast approaching a bridge. The rain must have made the road slick, for the car skidded, the driver lost control, and the car slammed into the side of the bridge!

The car came to a dead stop with the back end tottering dangerously over the water. Nonny and Tanta were stunned. The man and woman in front were seriously injured—she had a broken leg, and he was badly cut. As soon as they could free themselves, Nonny and Tanta attended to their injured friends. When the state police arrived, Nonny asked my great-aunt where baby Alfred was.

Was the tailor who had sewn my father's strong coat an angel in disguise?

Tanta responded, "I thought you had him!"

My great-grandmother wrung her hands and wailed, "Where's the baby?" He was nowhere to be seen.

Another car approached and stopped to help. From a vantage point behind the stranded car, someone was finally able to see my father—sound asleep through all the commotion—hanging by his coat-belt from a point on the rear of the car, suspended over the water far below.

Many years later, my father still remembers what it was like, having been retrieved from his precarious position, to stand there surrounded by the towering state policemen, Nonny, and his aunt. My great-grandmother was asking, "How will we get home now? We must be 25 or 30 miles from home, with no car and no driver!" At that very moment, two neighbors from Bridgeport, Mr. and Mrs. Scanzillo, drove up! In fact, they lived right next door to my great-grandmother.

"Don't worry, Mrs. Grasso," they told her. "We'll take you home."

Was the tailor who had sewn my father's strong coat an angel in disguise? Perhaps. And surely some divine force had led the neighbors to the crash site at just the right time. But most of all, I know now that, as my dad recalls, it was an invisible angel who rocked my young father to sleep and held him safely in place over the water until he could be rescued by human hands.

BY CARA GALLUCCI,
WITH ALFRED J. GALLUCCI, OF HINGHAM, MASSACHUSETTS

THANKS, JOE

◆ ◆ ◆

"BEE-YER, GETCHA ICE-COLD BEER!" The shouts echoed through Yankee Stadium. The scents of peanuts, popcorn, hot dogs, and a zillion other smells wafted along with the warm summer breeze as the crowd stood and roared expectantly. There was the man—long, lean, Joltin' Joe DiMaggio—stepping up to the plate. He was an unlikely hero for a demure little girl like me. But I hadn't a clue back then just how much of a hero Joe was going to be—for my son and my entire family.

Years later, my fourteen-year-old son Larry, the second of seven children, was an honor student, hometown baseball star, and an avid collector of baseball trivia. The game ruled his life, and everyone just knew this kid was going to make it to the majors. No doubt about it.

We were a baseball family back then. Three or four evenings a week, plus weekends, we'd all rush through an early dinner and head out to the ball-park for games or practice. Life was hectic, but grand.

An industrious boy, Larry took a job that summer to attend to his wants. One particular goal he achieved, after charming me out of my motherly objections, was the purchase of a ten-speed bike. He persuaded me that our Connecticut hills required all those speeds. I took his stated concern about my transportation woes with the proverbial grain of salt, but, as usual, I caved. He seemed so strong—so indestructible.

One afternoon, Larry took off on his beloved bike to go for a swim before work. He never took that swim. He never arrived at work.

Coming down a hilly, curving road, Larry and the bike hit a patch of sand. The bike stopped. Larry didn't. He sailed through the air, plummeted down a ravine, and hit a tree trunk—with his face.

Every blessed bone in his face, including the roof of his mouth, was broken, as well as each bone in his skull. Helmets for cyclists were unheard of back then.

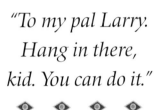

"To my pal Larry. Hang in there, kid. You can do it."

A month or so later, after several surgeries, our boy came home. He walked into the house—a tall, bald, disfigured skeleton—went into his room, and shut the door. Our family's collective heart broke as the days and weeks went by. Other than visits to various doctors, Larry never ventured out; no school chums were allowed in. We tried to engage him— oh, how we tried—but nothing worked.

The neurosurgeon told Larry, "No more contact sports, son, other than baseball, that is." I was horrified, but the doctor wisely explained that, while ball-playing might be dangerous for Larry, to take away that part of his life could be worse.

Time passed, and I soon found myself wanting him to play ball as, box by box and folder by folder, Larry's baseball treasures came out of his room. "Throw these away," he'd mumble through wired jaws, "I don't need them anymore." I took them, but didn't throw them away, hoping he'd eventually change his mind.

Late one afternoon, a close neighbor came by to visit our reclusive son. As the father of Larry's best friend, Russ passed muster and was allowed into Larry's increasingly private sanctuary. A short while later, Larry came bounding down the hall. "Mom! Dad!" he called excitedly. "Look at this, will ya!" He held up a large, inscribed photograph of Joe DiMaggio. "I gotta show this to Jimmy and Mike!" With that, he dashed out of the house and ran over the hill to find his buddies.

Bewildered at the sudden turn of events, I looked at Russ with raised eyebrows. We sat down, and Russ, a private jet pilot for a business magnate, explained about his latest flight. His only passenger that day had been one of the businessman's friends…Joe DiMaggio.

During the flight, Russ told the famous center fielder all about our son. After landing, and while still on the tarmac, Joe stopped, opened his briefcase, and handed Russ a photograph of himself with the inscription, "To my pal Larry. Hang in there, kid. You can do it." Russ noticed a single tear roll down Joe's face.

One compassionate droplet for an unknown boy's hopes and dreams—just one kind moment in a famous athlete's busy life generated a glorious rebirth for our child.

Once out of his dark shell, Larry went on to play baseball, attend college, and is now married with children of his own. That photograph of Joe still hangs on Larry's bedroom wall and smiles down at him every night. And every night, Larry smiles back.

Godspeed, Joe.

BY LYNNE ZIELINSKI

APRICOT ANGEL

◈ ◈ ◈

WHAT A WONDERFUL Father's Day get-together! Laughing, chattering, and singing, family and friends from all over the United States filled the patio of my in-laws' sunny Hemet, California, home. The "Hanson Family Trio"—my father-in-law, husband Don, and myself—accompanied the family on our instruments as they sang all their old favorite songs—everything from "Let Me Call You Sweetheart" to "The St. Louis Blues." Then, with 86-year-old "Dad" accompanying on a very mellow sax, Don's rich baritone soared out on a crowd-pleasing finale. Tired but exhilarated, we all lined up for a big buffet lunch.

"Here's your plate, Don," I called, holding out an empty one. But Don wasn't there. Surprised, I pushed through the crowd looking for him. Usually Don's towering head or booming voice make him easy to find. But this time he had completely disappeared. Fifteen minutes later, I finally found him—staggering out of the bathroom. He was in the middle of a massive heart attack.

After that, time seemed to freeze. Performing CPR, the rush to the hospital, long hours spent by Don's bedside or in the ICU waiting room, hurried doctor consultations, the heartbreak…everything was a blur. I was transfixed by the frightening machines over Don's bed with their relentless squiggles and beeps monitoring the 45 percent of his heart muscle that had survived. And, always, there was the waiting, the worrying, the praying.

By 11:30 A.M. the following Tuesday, I was in the depths of despair. I was only allowed to visit Don in the ICU for ten minutes at a time, and I didn't know if each hour—or minute—would be his last. *Oh, Don, what would I do without you?* I thought. *I'm so sorry....*

You see, the Saturday before, when we drove the 90 miles from our home in Orange County to Hemet for the Father's Day family reunion, I had fussed at Don the entire trip. At the baseball game we'd attended the night before, he'd been jumping up and twisting around so ridiculously, it had ruined my entire evening.

Now I was drowning in guilt. For Don's "gyrations" that night had been his attempts to shake off the pain of angina—heart attack warnings I'd been too irritated to discern. Now I felt genuinely awful, racked with anguish and despair. Oh, how I longed for someone to comfort me!

Of course, Don's folks came by to see him a couple times each day. But they were hosting that houseful of out-of-town visitors. Friends from home kept calling me on the waiting room pay phone, but they were all 90 miles away. One of my sons lived far up in northern California, and another was seriously ill with bronchitis. The third came from Los Angeles as often as he could, but that was two hours' drive each way. And I needed someone right then. Someone to hug me and assure me that everything was going to be all right.

"Dear Lord," I prayed, "I know this is impossible, but oh, I would so like to have a flesh-and-blood person right here in this room with me, to

> *"I know this is impossible, but oh, I would so like to have a flesh-and-blood person right here in this room with me, to hug me and hold my hand and pray with me!"*

hug me and hold my hand and pray with me!" Then, sighing, I stared through the window at the blistering desert sunshine outside.

About an hour later, the waiting room door pushed open. A young woman entered, looking around hesitantly. Her hair was tousled, perspiration dripped from her face, and stains covered her large apron. Very fresh, wet stains. Very orange stains. How embarrassing to be out in public looking like that!

"E-Excuse me," she stammered, "but, is anyone here waiting for a Mr. Don Hanson?"

"Why, yes!" I gasped. "I'm his wife, Bonnie. But—?"

She smiled shyly and held out her hand. "Hi, I'm April." Then she explained. "See, I live in Orange County. But I've been out here all week helping my mom can apricots. Just a while ago my husband called me from home. He said someone from Orange County named Don Hanson was critically ill here in the Hemet Hospital. 'Why don't you go over there and see if you can comfort his family?' he asked. So I set aside my pot of apricots, told Mom where I was going, jumped in the car, and here I am."

Glancing down at her apron, she gasped, "Oh, my, I am a sight, aren't I?" She whipped it off and gave me a big hug. Then she sat and prayed with me. How wonderful that felt! My guilt and fears were eased, and my heart felt a little lighter.

"Well, I better get back to my apricots before everything boils over!" April laughed. Another hug, and she was gone—before I even thought to ask her last name!

God had answered my prayer after all. Exactly the way I'd asked him to! Fortunately for me, my new friend didn't hesitate a moment when

God had answered my prayer after all. Exactly the way I'd asked him to!

God asked her to do something totally off-the-wall in the middle of canning a big pot of apricots!

My beloved husband did survive, and once again he's strong and full of life. How grateful we are for caring doctors, a loving family, and all our dear friends. I'm especially grateful to those friends we didn't even know we had. Because she listened to her heart when God prodded her, April, my "apricot angel," helped make my burdens easier to bear, so that I in turn could give even greater support to my husband.

Thank you, April!

BY BONNIE COMPTON HANSON

ANGEL ON FOUR LEGS

◆ ◆ ◆

NGELS, WE'VE BEEN TOLD, come in all shapes and sizes—
I know of one on four legs. He's a mixed collie/husky
dog with one of the most brave and angelic natures I've ever
encountered in an animal. I got him as a young pup one
autumn, but couldn't think of what to name him. Wandering around a
bookstore, hoping for inspiration, my hand hit a book that fell to the
floor. Looking down I saw the title: *Angels*. Angel became his name.

One of the reasons I'd decided to get a puppy was because my older
dog, Atalanta, though very attached to me, seemed lonely. Five years old,
Lannie (as I call her) was a large, striking lab/shepherd mix. The two dogs
quickly became inseparable. Both playful and protective, the dogs were a
comfort to each other and to me.

One day, a year and a half later, the dogs and I were outside enjoying
the cool spring weather. Suddenly, while leaping for a Frisbee, Lannie tore
the ligaments in both her back legs. Her scream of pain sliced through the
air, and Angel immediately rushed to her side. Lannie couldn't walk at all.
I had to carry her heavy hindquarters to the car and lift her inside.

I had just lost my job and my spirits were already low. Then the vet
informed me that an operation costing hundreds of dollars "might" save
my dog, but there were no guarantees. I took Lannie home and told her,
with love and determination in my voice, "Don't worry, we'll get you well.
God will help us."

*"Don't worry,
we'll get you well.
God will help us."*

I read up on her condition and learned that healing this kind of injury required both rest and movement. The legs could not be stressed, nor the ligaments strained further—and at the same time neither could be allowed to freeze up. At first, all I did was gently massage Lannie's legs every day, and I had to carry her hindquarters whenever she went out.

After a month, Lannie was able to hobble around. She still couldn't run or even walk normally, and after a few minutes she would tire and lay down, but I could see she was making progress.

I needed a way to let her exercise without putting weight on her legs, and I suddenly thought of the large creek running past the bottom of my backyard. Lannie loved to swim and would enthusiastically fetch sticks from the water. It was almost May, and in Maine that means the water is still pretty cold, but I knew it would be okay for a dog with a thick coat.

The previous summer, I had tried to get Angel into the water. I was sure he would like it and be a natural swimmer. But he wouldn't do it. He'd run along the bank and bark as Lannie dove in for a stick, but he would not go into the creek. After weeks of coaxing, I even tried to throw him in. He hit the water, panicked, sputtered, and lunged for shore. I felt so bad, I apologized to Angel and promised never to do it again.

The next sunny spring day, we all went down to the creek. I threw a stick into the water and Lannie went after it, as expected. As she swam for the stick, able to be active once again, her spirits seemed to soar.

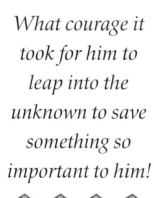

What courage it took for him to leap into the unknown to save something so important to him!

My idea worked well. Every day Lannie, Angel, and I went down to the creek. Lannie would fetch the stick for about 20 minutes, exercising her muscles and giving her ligaments a chance to realign and reattach in the weightless environment of water. Angel, meanwhile, was content to run back and forth along the bank.

Within mere weeks, Lannie had clearly improved. She was no longer hobbling. A few days passed when it rained so hard, we couldn't go down to the water. The next time we went, the creek had swollen quite a bit, but I didn't think much of it. The current was fast and there were rocks, but only out in the middle, about 40 feet away.

We began our regular ritual of tossing and fetching. After a few successful rounds, I threw the stick, but Lannie didn't see where it went. She began swimming around looking for it. She'd always been stubborn about retrieving, so even when I called to her she wouldn't give up. Swimming in increasingly wider arcs, Lannie was soon sucked into the current. Within seconds she was being pulled backward toward two big rocks. She managed to stabilize herself between the rocks while huge gushes of water poured over and around her, funneled by the hefty boulders. Lannie became a swimming machine fighting to get clear of the rocks and into the calmer water straight ahead of her. I raced along the bank trying frantically to get her to stop swimming and let the current carry her further back to more placid water, but she was focused ahead.

Angel watched the situation intently. I know he could feel my fear. Would Lannie tear her ligaments again, undoing all our patient healing? Or tiring, would she succumb to the current and be washed downstream to more dangerous rapids? The rocks, the rushing water, and deep mud in the shallows made it impossible for me to wade out to Lannie, though I attempted it several times. A good ten minutes passed, during which I never stopped calling to her.

Then a blur to my left caught my attention. It was Angel! He had sprung into the water, and with all his strength, he swam over to Lannie's side, grabbed her neck in his teeth, and jerked her out of the current. He then swam for shore while, stunned, I watched Lannie turn back and get caught in the current once again. Angel dragged himself up onto the bank, shook, and turned to greet his friend. The shock in his eyes as he discovered she was not with him was apparent. He looked up at me as if asking me to explain it. But he didn't question long. He plunged a second time into the creek and swam over to Lannie's side. Again, he sunk his teeth into her neck fur and yanked her free. His teeth still clenched onto Lannie's thick fur, Angel pulled her into calmer waters, refusing to release her until they were a few feet from the bank.

Out they crawled, dripping and shaking, while I laughed and danced around, praising Angel and comforting Lannie. That day, Angel lost his fear of the water. And over the next few weeks, with her best friend swimming beside her every day, Lannie made a complete recovery.

I was so proud of Angel for his heroic act, and I am still amazed remembering it. What courage it took for him to leap into the unknown to save something so important to him! Since that day, whenever I've had my own "leap into the unknown" to make, I've used Angel's example to give myself courage. He may have fur rather than feathery wings, but to me and Lannie, he's definitely our Angel.

BY ZOE CALDER

AN ANGEL WATCHING OVER ME

❖ ❖ ❖

Although I was only 11 years old, this day would be burned into my memory forever: It was the day I knew without a doubt that angels were watching over me.

THAT LONG-AGO DAY I remember looking up, seeing the sunlight dancing high above me through the greenish water mixed with silt from the lake's bottom. *I'll never make it,* I thought. As the rays of sunlight filtered through, I saw diamond sparkles swirling in the deep, and I recall thinking, *So this is what it's like to die.*

That summer morning at Meadowbrook Lake was typically hot and sticky. Although I was only 11 years old, this day would be burned into my memory forever: It was the day I knew without a doubt that angels were watching over me.

I spent the early morning at the edge of the lake with an oversized glass trying to swoop up a fish. First, I placed a ball of bread inside the glass and, while sitting in a foot of water, I eased the glass down. Then I waited until a curious fish swam in. Just as it did, I jerked my glass out of the water and—if I was quick enough—I'd catch a fish. I had played this game several times with Billy, a bully of a kid who lived near the lake, and I beat him every time. I could see the anger growing in his eyes, and I knew he was embarrassed that a girl had beaten him. Although it was obvious he was mad, I never dreamed how he would get even.

In the era of *Father Knows Best,* when most mothers stayed at home, my mother worked. Since my eight-year-old sister and I were often left alone, Mom occasionally drove us to the lake on summer mornings and picked us up after work. So that summer day my sister and I were on our own except for a few sunbathing families.

Tired of catching fish, I decided to sit on the sandy beach and build a sand castle. With the utmost care I built a moat around my castle and dribbled wet sand over the top of the steeples. My sister offered to make it pretty by sprinkling each steeple with dry white sand. About an hour later, we stood back and admired our handiwork.

In less than a heartbeat, I saw someone racing toward my newly made castle. Billy screamed "Geronimo!" as he jumped in the middle of it, scattering sand everywhere. I was so angry, I chased him across the beach and up the hill to the clubhouse. Then I lost sight of him. As the day wore on, I figured he'd gone home.

Feeling the burning sun on our backs, my sister and I found shelter beneath a sweet gum tree where we ate our sandwiches and potato chips. As we downed our sodas, we talked about the sand castle, its early demise, and how angry we were with Billy.

Easing back into the cool lake water, I showed my sister a perfect round of ten forward underwater flips. Squeezing water from my ponytail, I looked at my younger sister and said, "I bet I can swim out to the raft and back five times without stopping."

She grinned at me and said, "I bet you can't."

I was determined to show her I could do it. It was 500 yards out to the raft where the murky water stood more than 15 feet deep. I knew I could do it because I had mastered all the swimming strokes and even won a small trophy for the Australian crawl the year before.

As I continued my battle upward, I noticed diamond-like sparkles all around. They seemed to caress me. It was indescribably peaceful.

I took a deep breath and dove into the water. When I broke the surface, I eased into the Australian crawl, taking one easy stroke, then another, until I was effortlessly gliding through the water. I swam the crawl all the way out, touched the raft with my right hand, mentally said *One*, and then swam back to shore. Before my feet even touched bottom, I turned and started swimming back out. My arms felt heavy, so I turned over and began to float, letting my kicking legs carry me to the raft's side.

"Two," I said triumphantly, as I touched the side of the raft. Since no one was on the raft, I kicked off powerfully from its side, causing it to sway. My breathing became ragged and I slowed it by swimming on my side. When I reached shore again, I glanced toward the beach. When I didn't see my sister, I stood there for a few seconds catching my breath.

Well, I thought, *three times out there and back is not too shabby.* I shielded my eyes against the glaring sun and looked at the faraway raft. The raft was still empty. After a long, deep breath, I began the crawl once more.

As I neared the raft, I heard someone splashing near me. Before I knew it, Billy's face was inches from mine as he grabbed the top of my head with both hands. He shoved me under. Already winded, I fought to reach air. As I broke the water's surface, I gasped, and air as cool as a mountain stream rushed in. Then Billy pushed me under again.

This time it was harder to reach the surface. My arms and legs felt like heavy weights. I struggled, kicking as hard as I could to once more fill my lungs with the sweet taste of air. As I reached the surface I tried to swim to the raft, but Billy was back in my face again.

He gritted his teeth, his eyes flashing anger. I flailed my arms at him trying to get away. But with both hands on top of my head, he thrust me under the water again. Then he pushed me farther under with his feet until he was almost standing on my shoulders.

With my lungs about to burst, I began kicking, trying desperately to reach the water's surface. But the struggle had exhausted me, and this time I didn't know if I could make it back up. Time slowed to a crawl. Everything seemed to be moving in a slow-motion dance—including me.

I remember looking up, seeing the sunlight quivering high above me through the hazy water. *I'll never make it,* I thought. As I continued my battle upward, I noticed diamond-like sparkles all around. They seemed to caress me. It was indescribably peaceful. I recall thinking, *So this is what it's like to die.* It was so beautiful and comforting beneath the water that I was almost content to stay there. But God had other plans for me.

I broke through the water gasping wildly. I couldn't seem to get enough air into my aching lungs. Then I heard someone calling from the raft, "Give me your hand!" I stretched toward the voice. A man caught my hand and dragged me toward the raft just seconds before Billy reached me again. With one last angry splash at me, Billy turned and swam back to shore. On the raft, I sat for what seemed an eternity, spitting up water and gasping. *Where did this man come from?* I wondered.

I know, for a fact, there was no one on the raft as I swam out. Yet when my life was in mortal danger, a man seemed to appear from nowhere.

I'll never really know how the man got there, but I do know that God commands angels to guard his children. A lifetime later, I still don't know whether the man was sent from heaven or not, but it doesn't really matter. I had an angel who was watching over me.

BY NANETTE SNIPES

OUR LITTLE ANGEL

◆ ◆ ◆

O UR DAUGHTER Robin's pregnancy had been difficult from the start. We were getting increasingly worried because she and her husband lived two hours from the nearest hospital. In the final months, her doctor advised the young mother-to-be to stay with us, her parents, in town near the hospital. Robin readily agreed. Complications could develop. The baby could come quickly. We all knew the risks, but we tried to focus on the result for which we had prayed: the arrival of Robin's first baby, our second grandchild.

My wife, Shirley, and I urged Robin to rest as we went about operating our small neighborhood convenience store. The morning the baby was born started like many others. I was up at 6:00 A.M. to open the store. Shirley was sleeping, until she heard Robin's anxious call. "Mom, Mom," Robin whispered. "I'm sorry to wake you, but I think my water broke."

The baby is coming, Shirley realized, instantly awake and remembering the doctor's warnings that everything could happen very quickly. Not reaching the hospital in time could endanger both Robin and the baby. "Don't worry," Shirley urged, fighting to sound calm even though her heart was pounding. "Just get ready and we'll go. I'll tell Dad."

I closed up the store and started the car. Shirley dressed hurriedly and went to check on Robin. She was in the tub. Not wanting to alarm her, Shirley hadn't passed along all the doctor's warnings. Now, as she tried to hurry the ungainly mother-to-be, she wished she had.

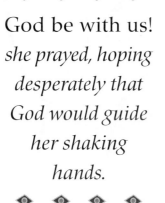

◆ ◆ ◆ ◆

God be with us!
*she prayed, hoping
desperately that
God would guide
her shaking
hands.*

◆ ◆ ◆ ◆

Precious minutes ticked away as Robin looked for the nightgown she had planned to bring and chose an outfit for the baby to wear home. Labor pains hadn't really started except for some twinges, but Shirley knew that didn't matter. Finally, Shirley couldn't stand it any more. "We have to go right now!" she said.

By then, Robin had begun to feel some stronger contractions. As we drove the nearly empty streets toward the hospital, the pains began coming one after another. Robin cried out in anguish, and I tried to concentrate on the road. As she attempted to soothe and reassure Robin, Shirley prayed. *God be with us! God be with us!* Shirley, who had always relied on her strong faith, repeated the prayer over and over.

Finally, I turned into the hospital drive and headed toward a lighted sign that said "Emergency." I had hoped to see white-coated attendants running out to meet us as they did on television. But the area looked deserted. I stopped the car and dashed for the door. It was locked! A sign said to use another entrance before 7:00 A.M. I checked my watch: It was 6:45. I had no idea where to go.

Shirley had opened the rear car door to help Robin out, but she couldn't get off the backseat. "It's too late, Mom," she sobbed. "The baby's coming."

Shirley kneeled next to the car and prepared herself to deliver the baby. *God be with us! God be with us!* she prayed, hoping desperately that God would guide her shaking hands. She could see the top of the baby's head. Then she saw the umbilical cord wrapped around its tiny neck, tightening with each contraction.

Oh, Lord. What do I do now? Shirley thought, terrified.

Just then, she felt a rush of air and heard something like the sound of flapping wings. She raised her eyes to see an angel hovering gracefully above Robin. She blinked, but the beautiful, winged creature remained, smiling back at her.

To her own amazement, Shirley suddenly knew what to do. She calmly ordered Robin to stop pushing and deftly untangled the cord. In seconds, she was holding her wailing grandson. But Shirley knew the danger wasn't over. The complications the doctor had warned her about still threatened. We had to get help immediately.

♦ ♦ ♦ ♦

"God heard my prayer and sent his angels to help us."

♦ ♦ ♦ ♦

Frantic, I pounded on the emergency room doors, but didn't see anyone. I turned to run around the building and search for an open door. That's when I noticed the man in the white jacket.

"They're coming," the man said serenely. "Wait just a moment more, and they'll be here. Everything will be fine."

"Are you a doctor?" I started to ask. But just then, the doors burst open, and a pair of nurses rushed out. They ran for a gurney and wheeled Robin and the baby inside. *The man must have alerted the staff,* I thought, and I turned to thank him. But the fellow was gone.

Stunned and exhausted, Shirley and I waited silently to hear whether our daughter and grandson would be all right. In her mind, Shirley recalled the image of the angel. She knew without a doubt that everything would be fine. I wondered about that stranger and wished I could tell him how much his help had meant to us.

Robin's doctor had arrived by then. The smile on his face as he approached told us all we needed to know. "Are you folks trying to put me out of business?" the obstetrician teased.

"Not on your life. I never want to do anything like that again," Shirley declared.

Not until later did my wife and I discuss all that had happened. I listened, shocked, as Shirley described the angel. The stranger suddenly took on a new significance. "I wonder if…" I hesitated to finish the thought.

But Shirley knew instantly what had happened. Tears welled up in her eyes as she said, "God heard my prayer and sent his angels to help us."

Our grandson, Julian, a happy boy, turns 13 years old this summer. Shirley says, "Every time I see him, I thank God again. He's our little angel."

BY PHIL CONTINO

AN AMBASSADOR OF HOPE

❖ ❖ ❖

ERHAPS THERE WAS NEVER a more aptly named entertainer than Bob Hope. For nearly 50 years, he used his gift of joke-telling to bring hope and cheer to military troops stationed in difficult situations around the world.

Hope has entertained troops overseas in every war from World War II to the Gulf War. The news media called him "America's #1 Soldier in Greasepaint," and the soldiers dubbed him "G.I. Bob." Hope, as a messenger of cheer, began his "mission" in March 1941 when he traveled with a group of Hollywood performers to March Field, California, to do a radio show for military personnel stationed there. His first trip into a combat area was in 1943 during World War II when he and a small group of USO entertainers encouraged troops in England, Africa, Sicily, and Iceland. In peacetime, Hope continued his visits to military bases and veteran's hospitals.

In 1948, Bob Hope began his Christmas-show custom when he went to Germany to entertain military personnel involved in the Berlin airlift. Although Hope announced during a 1972 show in Vietnam that he'd no longer be doing Christmas shows, he just couldn't stay away. Year after year, Hope continued his tradition of going wherever soldiers faced the lonely holidays far from loved ones.

Hope went to Beirut in 1983. In 1987 he flew around the world to the Pacific, Atlantic, and Indian oceans and then to the Persian Gulf. His

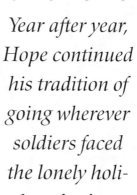

❖ ❖ ❖ ❖

Year after year, Hope continued his tradition of going wherever soldiers faced the lonely holidays far from loved ones.

❖ ❖ ❖ ❖

Goodwill Tour in 1990 took him to England, Russia, and Germany. The tour's grand finale was in Saudi Arabia, where Hope offered his "cup of Christmas cheer" to the men and women of Operation Desert Storm.

Bob Hope, born on May 29, 1903, is well into his nineties now. But he continues to tell his jokes. Although he has recently retired from making his global treks to cheer the troops, there is no doubt that for years to come, he will remain an icon of hope to those whose lives he has touched.

Don Morley, one of the many soldiers inspired by Hope, shares his personal experience and reflects on how much this beloved funnyman meant to wartime troops:

"At a time when lots of guys were being drafted into the military to fight in the Vietnam War, I enlisted in the U.S. Marine Corps. My actual tour of duty in Nam was from August 1968 to September 1969, during which time I worked behind enemy lines to intercept communication. However, it was just before my tour (during my three-and-a-half months of training as a Morse Code Intercept Operator), that I had the opportunity to see one of Bob Hope's live shows.

"I had finished my ten weeks of boot camp and eight weeks of infantry training in Southern California. Lots of the guys from infantry training had been sent to Nam right away. The rest of us went on to get Military Occupational Specialty (MOS) training at an old airbase in Pensacola, Florida.

"If you've ever been in the military, you know it's hard to maintain morale. Whether you're overseas or stateside, you're feeling a lot of

ANGELS ALL AROUND

homesickness, loneliness, and desolation all rolled into one. And as for us, we knew the Vietnam War was raging, and we knew we'd all probably be going over there. Everyone was in that 'military mode.' We were just trying to get by until we reached the better days we hoped were ahead of us. Somehow, I think Bob Hope knew that. I think he knows how military people feel when they're away from home.

"Not too many people are aware that Bob Hope did stateside military shows as well as shows overseas, but he did, and it was a high point for us just hearing the announcement that he was coming to Pensacola. Once we knew about it, it was a struggle to concentrate on what we were supposed to be doing. Any free time we had, we'd go watch the stage crew putting everything up. There was a lot of anticipation in the air.

"Compared with a lot of the large military bases, Pensacola was just a small, obscure place. But Bob showed up there with a full-scale production. There was a 100-foot stage, a full orchestra, a band, everything. It was a complete traveling show, and it was big.

"The show itself was really exciting. There was a wide range of entertainment, something to appeal to everybody. And Bob, of course, would let himself be roasted by every guest. That was his shtick. It was hilarious. There were thousands of us in the risers and bleachers, and the energy level was tremendous. There were guys screaming, yelling, and cheering. Hats were flying in the air. The show was so well done, so professionally put together. Bob is not a halfway kind of guy; he's a perfectionist, and his show reflected that.

"To me, the best thing about it, though, was that Bob Hope brought a little bit of home to everybody, a little of the backyard. And for just that

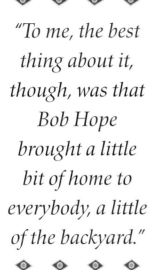

"To me, the best thing about it, though, was that Bob Hope brought a little bit of home to everybody, a little of the backyard."

176 ◆ *WHISPERS FROM HEAVEN*

little while, you weren't in the military, you weren't worrying about what your sergeant was going to say, you weren't worried about where you were going to go, what duty station you were going to pull, what order you were going to get cut. For those couple of hours, you were just watching a great show.

"Bob Hope knew he had the talent and ability to entertain people, and so he did, but you've got to remember that when he entertained military troops, he didn't get paid for any of it. When anyone went on a USO show, it was totally voluntary. And some of the other places Bob went overseas—into war zones—required a big risk on his part. It took a lot of grit, bravery, and fortitude to go into those places and put on those shows.

"I think Bob Hope is one of the greatest comedians who has ever lived. I honestly believe that. He really has a heart for people. Even if you watch his old movies, you can see the compassion in him. He cares about people. And he's definitely had a heart for the military people away from home, knowing that they were lonely, that they hurt inside, and that they needed something. Bob Hope could definitely entertain you; he could put a smile on your face. But more than that, he put a smile in your heart."

BY CHRISTINE DALLMAN

WHEN ANGELS KISS

◇ ◇ ◇

*A*S A LITTLE GIRL, my favorite Bible story was that of Samuel, the boy who heard God's voice. I was only about four years old the first time I heard it in Sunday school, but I remember how badly I wanted to hear God call my name, too. I would lie awake in bed, straining my ears to filter out the night sounds of ticking clocks, crickets, creaking floor boards, and my father's snoring. I wondered what God's voice would sound like. Would it be a booming shout or a quiet whisper? Would I still be awake when he called to me, or would it happen at night while I was sleeping? I never imagined it would take 40 years to finally learn the answers to my questions.

It was a beautiful Sunday morning in August, so clear and free of humidity that the air sparkled. This day was my 44th birthday. It was also the day my mother died. She had only been ill for two weeks, and as a health care worker, I knew what could have happened, so I was grateful she went peacefully. But as her daughter, I was tormented with thoughts that maybe there was something I had overlooked; something that, had I caught it in time, could have saved my mother.

That night was one of the hardest of my life. I found no solace in the company of others, though I knew my sister was grieving, too. All we had now was each other, and I felt terribly alone. I prayed through the night that God would help me, and although I didn't hear him answer, he did.

◇ ◇ ◇ ◇

What I didn't realize was that this whole time God was whispering in my ear, but I wasn't hearing him … yet.

◇ ◇ ◇ ◇

Over the following days, I worked on a tribute for the memorial service. Finding the right words was not difficult, since Mom had been a strong Christian woman up to the end. But I knew I could add some special touches by looking in her Bible. She had always told me, "Remember, everything's written in here." I had never opened her Bible before because I thought of it as her personal property, like a pocketbook or a diary. Now I would have to look inside to find where she had noted her favorite hymns and passages. Afraid it would start me crying again, my hands trembled as I opened it. But my fear of sorrow dissolved as I read what she had written, and a blanket of peace began to settle over me.

Next to different verses, Mom had jotted down the names of family and friends, as happy reminders or promises to pray for them. In the margins were dates, observations, and the chronology of her Christian journey. I was surprised to learn she had become a Christian at the age of 44, the same age I turned the day she died. It was like the completion of a cycle for me, learning that we shared a "birthday" of sorts. What I didn't realize was that this whole time God was whispering in my ear, but I wasn't hearing him…yet.

As time passed, fear started poking through my sorrow. How was I going to pay all the bills and maintain the house on my own? What if a major appliance or the car broke down? What if I became sick or lost my job? I was giving a lot of public lip service to God, saying he would take care of me, but privately my worry was gnawing away at me.

Then, one morning on my way out the door, an object in the corner of the kitchen caught my eye: a little antique chalkboard. It had hung on the wall there for years, used for memos, grocery lists, and baking times. Taking it for granted, I hadn't noticed the words written on it before. Now the chalk nearly leapt off the old scratched slate. In my mother's neat handwriting, these words were written: "Jesus is a Way Maker" and "Jesus Never Fails." My heart skipped a beat when I read them. I felt like Samuel! Through my mother, God had spoken to me, and I had finally heard him.

I resolved never to wipe those words from the slate, and from that day on, I started noticing other things that gave me pause and confirmed what I was slowly learning: God's voice is everywhere.

The following spring, I was walking down the driveway to the mailbox when I saw something shining among the stones and gravel. Thinking it to be a piece of metal that had dropped from the recycling bin, I bent to pick it up. To my amazement, I found myself holding a small pair of praying hands. They had been my mother's, and I had lost them eight months prior, on the day of her memorial service. They had been there through the winter, in rain and snow, driven over countless times. Yet, incredibly, here they were, shiny as new, safe in my palm, a reminder of God's love.

Less than a month later, I came home from work to find another curious sight. I had previously set some small porcelain cherubs on a chair by the back door. Now two of them had fallen over, one on its back, the other kneeling over it, their faces locked in a kiss. There was no wind; it had been a calm day. My first thought was "Mom." It was the playful sort of thing she would have done. My sister said the same thing when I described the little angels to her. "Mom visited you," she said.

Bluebirds, the traditional sign of happiness and good fortune, were always just a fleeting sight for us on their migratory route each spring and fall. But since my mom died, a family of four have lived in my yard year-round. There are no feeders or birdhouses to attract them, but every day I see a bit of bright blue cheer flitting in the trees and across the lawn. To me, the birds represent my family—my parents, my sister, and myself—and they remind me that we'll all be together again one day.

Living in the country, I've always enjoyed the quiet nights, sitting outside watching the stars. There are times when I lose sight and forget my chalkboard's messages. I feel sad when I can't afford a movie rental on a Saturday night because there's only ten dollars left between now and next payday. But then I'll see a brilliant streak of light arc across the sky and remember I'm not alone. Watching a magnificent meteor shower, nature's fireworks, fills me with awe—and it's free!

What took me so long to learn was that the gift I'd wanted for so many years had always been there. I just wasn't ready to accept it. Now I know God's voice can be heard at any time in a variety of ways, whether it's loud as thunder or soft as an angel's kiss. All the things I had filtered out were part of God's voice trying to get in. His voice is like mixed-media artwork: a symphony played to the northern lights wrapped in a garden painted in gold. He's been talking to me all along. But now I've learned to "listen" with all my senses.

One day not too long ago, a beautiful, perfectly heart-shaped cloud drifted across the sky. I smiled as it passed and whispered back, "I love you, too."

BY DEBY MURRAY

What took me so long to learn was that the gift I'd wanted for so many years had always been there. I just wasn't ready to accept it.

JOURNEY TO RECOVERY

◇ ◇ ◇ ◇

THEY TOOK AWAY what should have been my eyes,
(But I remembered Milton's Paradise).
They took away what should have been my ears,
(Beethoven came and wiped away my tears).
They took away what should have been my tongue,
(But I had talked with God when I was young).
He would not let them take away my soul—
Possessing that, I still possess the whole.

—HELEN KELLER

ELLIE

❖ ❖ ❖

This story is
about my sister,
but it's also the
story of one of
those journeys—
those countless,
commonplace,
and astounding
journeys that
families, together,
often make.

LLIE WAS THE BABY of the Thrift family, heir to the extra attention and wistful hugs that the youngest child usually gets. Even today, all grown up, she sometimes remembers she's the baby and plays it for all it's worth. She is clever, funny, and loyal, with wisdom far beyond her years. And even if she hadn't drawn that cherished last-born spot, Ellie would have affected our family in a very special way.

I was the firstborn in this family of girls and was almost four when Margie, the middle child, came along. Margie was a beautiful baby with a creamy complexion and soft, dark ringlets; she was, as I heard over and over, "all Thrift." I was too, of course, but next to this small, dark cherub, I loomed pale and freckled. Worse, she was a good baby who sucked her thumb and played quietly while I—as the story goes—tore through the house leaving family heirlooms in shards. Margie was the kind of baby you wanted to pinch, and I'm sorry to say I probably did, more than once.

When Ellie was born in the spring of '56, there were many hurried phone calls, and Margie and I, then three and seven, were packed off to stay with an aunt. Our baby sister would be fine, we were assured, but first she would need an operation. Our parents told us we would enjoy Aunt Margaret's farm in the Blue Ridge Mountains, and, except for missing them and wondering about the new baby, we did.

The farm had everything a child could wish for—horses, cows, cats and dogs, fields and woods, a tiny cement pond littered with blooms of pink mimosa, stables and barns, and a wood-paneled tack room that smelled of leather. We rode horseback with our older girl cousins down winding country roads: Margie sat cradled in front of Caroline, while I clung precariously behind Carla. We followed the boys, Ross and John, up the steep ladder to their tree house where Margie cut her foot on a rusty nail and everyone scowled at her because the tree house was declared off-limits until Uncle Paul could make it safe. We fed corn to Caroline's chestnut gelding until we thought his stomach would burst, and I fell in love with an Appaloosa foal and dreamed that he would be mine. In the evenings, Margie fell asleep sucking her thumb while my aunt read to the rest of us from *Pinocchio*. Two months passed, and we started lobbying to go home. "Soon," my aunt would say. "Your sister is almost ready to go home from the hospital."

When we went back home, our mother had moved us into the big bedroom so the new baby could have the smaller one. We'd been told that our little sister had needed an operation "on her nose." This was a short and gentle way to explain the cleft palate and double cleft lip that had robbed Ellie of the middle of her face. While Margie and I had played in the country, Ellie had spent her first spring at Johns Hopkins, where surgeons worked miracles to repair the damage nature had capriciously wrought.

"She's cute!" we squealed when we saw her, and she was. At three months old, Ellie's soft brown eyes were alight with the promise of future mischief. Her fine fuzzy hair glowed reddish-brown. Her new nose was flat and wide, and her upper lip was criss-crossed with fine, dark lines. She immediately replaced the foal in my heart, and I don't think even Margie, whose turn it was to feel usurped, was jealous.

Like all babies, Ellie had to eat every few hours, but she couldn't suck with the new, healing lip, so my mother had to feed her with a medicine dropper. "Just like a baby bird," Mother sometimes said. An injured baby bird she was, too, cuddled and loved and coaxed to good health. My mother fed her with the medicine dropper day and night for nearly a year, mixing strained baby foods into a thick formula as Ellie grew.

For 18 months, there was no roof in this baby's mouth, and when she ate, food was sometimes pushed up and out of her nose. It is only now, after I have mothered three babies myself, babies who could be fed in the normal fashion, that I truly appreciate my mother's patience and strength. Ellie's second operation came with her second Christmas. Santa Claus visited the hospital, and when Ellie came home on New Year's Day it was with a new roof in her mouth—her food would now go down more easily.

Perhaps it was because my parents were so committed to doing everything they could for Ellie, or perhaps it was because Ellie so matter-of-factly accepted these trials, that getting ready for her annual summertime stays at Johns Hopkins seemed almost like getting ready for camp. Maybe it was because this ritual became our family's summer routine—in lieu of vacations—for so many years. Mother would make Ellie new pajamas, someone would give her a present, and with a favorite toy (such as Elewent the elephant) and some books to color or read, everything would be packed into her small suitcase. For my mother, it was probably not at all like sending a child to camp, but she kept things so cheerful, it almost seemed like Ellie was heading someplace fun.

JOURNEY TO RECOVERY

It did not seem like camp to Ellie, either, though she told me later it was years before she realized it was only she who went to the hospital each year, not everyone else. When she was older, nightgowns replaced pajamas, Barbie replaced Elewent, and Ellie came home with the names of roommates who then became pen pals.

I remember trips to Johns Hopkins in Baltimore: the hot, heavy air pushing through the open windows of our '55 Ford, the people fanning themselves on rowhouse stoops in street after street, mile after mile of the dirty, rundown neighborhoods that surrounded the pristine hospital. I remember sitting with my silent father in a dingy restaurant on one such street eating salty, tasteless soup and not having anything to say.

Once, when she was three or four, Ellie was sent home from the hospital with a half ring of steel taped to her face to protect her newly sculpted features. The ring stuck out in front of her nose and lip, and in her eyes I glimpsed an unsure, wounded look. At first it was so wrenching to see her like this that Margie and I treated her with special kindness, but after several days the three of us had accepted it enough to stage a bullfight with Ellie as the bull. Then the itching under the tape became unbearable, and Ellie yanked the ring off.

In old family photos, Ellie grins into the Brownie camera, her expression sometimes sweet, sometimes shy, but from her eyes there is always the unmistakable glint of mischief. It manifested itself in various ways: Ellie riding naked up the hill on her little tricycle, sitting on a pillowcase snatched from the clothesline to protect her bare bottom from the cold metal seat; Ellie sprinkling a winding trail of Comet cleanser through the house while she pretended to be Hansel and Gretel; Ellie sneaking a loaf

When she was older, nightgowns replaced pajamas, Barbie replaced Elewent, and Ellie came home with the names of roommates who then became pen pals.

of raisin bread off the Wonder truck and emerging later from under the forsythia bush with a stomachache and an empty plastic bag.

When she was 14, Ellie was pixie cute, with big, golden-brown eyes that danced in a heart-shaped face. Her skin was creamy and smooth, and only the scars on her upper lip hinted at anything out of the ordinary. Her chestnut hair grew long and thick, with natural waves that defied attempts at straightening. One of her friends suggested that the hair was a clue to Ellie's nature: stubborn.

It's true. Under Ellie's graceful exterior, she had tremendous strength. People were often surprised that this gentle girl not only thought for herself, but sometimes came to conclusions that challenged convention. But though she would defend her own values if need be, she never tried to convince anyone that they ought to see things her way. At 14, her laugh was still full of mischief, yet this same kid taped *It Pays to Increase Your Word Power* on the bathroom mirror so she could learn while brushing her teeth. Even I, a self-absorbed young adult, could see that Ellie had a depth about her that most of the rest of us simply didn't have.

That year, her doctors at Johns Hopkins gave her a choice: She could continue with one or more surgeries—cosmetic only from here on out—or she could stop going to the hospital and spend her summers someplace else. My parents and her doctors left the decision up to her. All 13 surgeries had been successful: Her mouth and nose worked well and looked fine. Speech therapy had ensured there were no speech problems, and the challenging dental needs caused by the cleft itself and subsequent reconstructions were being superbly, if not painlessly, met by specialists at the National Institutes of Health. I think we all expected that

People were often surprised that this gentle girl not only thought for herself, but sometimes came to conclusions that challenged convention.

Ellie would continue, not that we thought she needed it—she looked absolutely wonderful to us and "normal" to others, I'm sure. But normal is not perfect, and who, especially a teenager, would turn down the chance to be perfect?

The miracle of modern plastic surgery is a legacy of World War II. Fixing the casualties of war had spurred the science to heights never before approached. Had Ellie been born even ten years sooner, her fate would have been a crude repair job, and the severity of her particular case would have left her with debilitating speech impediments. We had been fortunate to live within driving distance of the leading medical schools and research institutions in the country.

Now, with just a few more operations, the minor scarring on Ellie's upper lip would be erased, and the nose that was just a trifle thick for such a delicate face could be perfected.

But Ellie chose to stop. Perhaps she had been through enough pain. Perhaps, as our mother suggests, she had developed a great patience through all the years and trials that gave her a unique insight into what is important and what is not. Or perhaps, unlike many who spend so much time and effort trying to correct all that is not perfect, Ellie was happy to have achieved near-perfection.

What is perfection, anyway? Is it something any of us could ever hope to achieve? Better to strive for wholeness, toward a self-love that accepts even flaws. Like Ellie, we can acknowledge our progress, appreciate the simple pleasures of life, and get on with living, embracing ourselves and others for being the imperfect, yet beautiful, people we are.

BY DIANA THRIFT

JERRY SCHEMMEL'S STORY
Surviving a Plane Crash Was Just the Beginning

◆ ◆ ◆

ON JULY 19, 1989, United Airlines Flight 232 out of Denver, Colorado, crashed in Sioux City, Iowa. It was a scene played repeatedly on national television. To see it, one wonders how anyone could have lived through it. Of approximately 290 people onboard, more than 100 perished, but, miraculously, over 180 people made it through the ordeal alive. Jerry Schemmel was one of those survivors, and it changed his life forever.

Jerry was the deputy commissioner and legal counsel of the Continental Basketball Association. Jay Ramsdell, his good friend and boss, was the commissioner. The two were on their way to the CBA's college draft in Columbus, Ohio, with a stopover in Chicago.

Running late, they rushed to Denver's old Stapleton Airport only to find that their 7:00 A.M. flight had been canceled—and the next four flights were filled. Jerry and Jay were put on standby. At 12:45 in the afternoon, they got the last two available seats onboard United Airlines Flight 232. Jerry was given a ticket in Row 23, and Jay was issued a ticket in Row 30. The noisy plane was filled to the brim. Over north-central Iowa, about 150 miles from Sioux City, the unthinkable happened. There was an onboard explosion. Engine number two was wiped out, taking with it the entire hydraulic system. The plane should have been unflyable, but against all odds, the cockpit crew managed to regain some control of the crippled aircraft.

"The plane was veering to the right and circled the small airport in Sioux City 13 times. We came in with an air speed of 255 mph. The normal landing for a DC-10 is 125 mph. The rate of descent was ten times the normal amount," Jerry recalls. "We were told 45 minutes before impact to expect to crash, and there was very little confidence for landing safely and walking off."

Right before they hit, he remembers the cockpit captain announcing to the passengers, "I'm not going to kid anybody—this is going to be rough. This is going to be tougher than anything you've ever been through." Thirty seconds before touchdown, the captain gave the command, "Brace, brace, brace."

"The plane hit the edge of the runway with its right wing first. There was a lot of chaos—bodies being thrown about, smoke and fire, unrecognizable debris being thrown everywhere. The plane then cartwheeled forward and slid upside down and broke apart, veering into a cornfield."

Jerry was hanging upside down, still strapped in his seat, when his part of the plane came to rest. Badly shaken, Jerry had no idea whether he was dead or alive. Only when fire burned a knuckle on his hand did he fully realize that he had survived. Unbuckling his seat belt, he dropped onto the ceiling, which was now the floor.

As he backed away from the fire, he heard two men behind him. One of them said, "Let's start helping some people and maybe we can find a way out in the process." As the three began helping other survivors, they

"When I got out, I heard a baby crying. The next thing I knew, I was back inside the wreckage."

glimpsed a ray of sunlight through the smoke and inched their way out of the plane.

Jerry says that what happened next was a matter of instinct. "When I got out, I heard a baby crying. The next thing I knew, I was back inside the wreckage." He found an 11-month-old girl wedged inside an overhead compartment. "I gathered her up and ran back outside thinking the plane would explode, which was the first time I weighed the risk of what I did."

Unfortunately, Jerry's friend, Jay Ramsdell, did not survive. He had been sitting in Row 30, which was about where the plane had broken apart. It took four days to identify his body.

Jerry recovered physically, but he battled post-traumatic stress disorder, anguishing through overwhelming periods of guilt and depression. Jay had died, as had a one-year-old boy sitting in front of Jerry. Before the explosion, Jerry had been playing peekaboo with the child. The randomness—and unfairness—of who lived and who died haunted him. He couldn't feel grateful for his life because he felt guilty for being alive.

His career, which had once been the most important thing in his life, seemed pointless. He was in a downward spiral and couldn't see a glimmer of hope. He stopped returning phone calls, even to his family.

His wife, Diane, had unwavering Christian faith. When she encouraged Jerry to reach out to God, he shut her out. But her consistent strength and courage slowly began to touch his heart. He found himself wondering if God could help him.

"I was sitting in my chair one evening, ten months after the crash, when I realized, for the first time in my life, I couldn't get back up on my own," Jerry admits. At that low point, with no answers in sight, he began

For ten months Jerry had been longing for rest, and now he realized that Jesus promised to provide it.

to pray. He asked God to help him, to come into his life and to lift him back up.

Jerry also started reading the Bible. He read a passage in Matthew that pierced his loneliness and calmed his fears: "Come to me all you who labor and are heavy laden, and I will give you rest." For ten months Jerry had been longing for rest, and now he realized that Jesus promised to provide it.

With that verse firmly planted in his mind, Jerry turned the corner away from the crash and toward all that God had planned for him. His priorities changed. Christian convictions and focusing on Jesus replaced career goals. His family took priority over his once all-consuming job.

Jerry is now the voice of the Denver Nuggets, and doing play-by-play is still incredibly exciting for him. But whether they win or lose is now way down on his list of things that matter.

Jerry says he goes back to that life-changing Bible passage every day, and he remembers the relief that flooded over him when he let Jesus lift his burden. It took a plane crash to open his eyes and his heart to the love and rest that Jesus can bring. He hopes it won't take such dire circumstances for others to find it as well.

BY RICH BRIGGS

LEARNING TO DANCE

❖ ❖ ❖

MY FAMILY CELEBRATES our special occasions in a big way. No matter what's going on, we ALL celebrate. This particular occasion was my sister's graduation from a small midwestern college. It was a wonderful institution that had made all of us feel comfortable and welcome, from Karen's orientation to the commencement invitation.

We planned this event for weeks. Dad called AAA to be sure we had the most up-to-date route and to guarantee that no roadwork would deter us. Mom began organizing the rest of our family to make sure all calendars were cleared and everyone was aware of the date. She also baked—as she usually does—her special chocolate chip cookies. There were enough to feed us for the five-hour trip, and a surplus to pass around to Karen's dormitory pals.

The day finally arrived. We loaded up the car and headed off to Karen's college commencement. There was endless anticipation, endless chatter, and an endless supply of chocolate chip cookies. The five-hour trip took at least two days, in my mind. But eventually we were barreling up the stairs of Karen's dorm and running to her room.

The excitement was contagious, and none of us could stop talking. Karen joined us as we drove to our hotel and checked in. Once we were all settled, we stopped at the information office of the college and picked up our itinerary for the weekend. There was not much time to spare,

What should have been a wonderful and joyous day of celebration turned, for me, into a depressing situation. I knew I would not be able to dance that night.

since the president's reception began that evening at 5:30, and it was already 4:00. We had enough time to change from crinkled travel clothes into dressy casual attire and be right on time. The reception was as warm and personal as always. Afterward, we headed for our favorite family restaurant, with Karen basking in the glow of her big day. We took time to figure out the rest of the weekend and found commencement scheduled for 10:00 A.M., a pickup softball game at 3:00, and the famous rock revival dance, which we were all excited about, scheduled for 8:00 on Saturday evening.

Everything was a whirlwind of activity. Saturday morning arrived quickly, and Karen looked jubilant in her graduation robe. We took pictures and hugged and cried, the perfect example of a loving midwestern family.

At the pickup game that afternoon, everyone played except Mom, who claimed she got more enjoyment out of watching. I slammed my first pitch toward center field and headed for first base. Apparently, the hit was not as long as I thought it was: The ball and I were both headed for first base at the same time. In order to beat the tag, I decided to slide. I got to the base first, but my right foot twisted in a different direction from the rest of my leg. I didn't think it was a real problem until I had to run for second base. What should have been a dash turned into a limp.

Dad helped me off the diamond, and we struggled to the college medical center. A poke, a probe, and an X ray revealed that nothing was broken. However, it required a wrap and a pair of crutches. What should have been a wonderful and joyous day of celebration turned, for me, into a depressing situation. I knew I would not be able to dance that night.

Not only was I limping and using crutches, but I couldn't even get a shoe over the bulky bandage on my ankle. Try though I might, I just couldn't muster up much enthusiasm for the dance. I love to dance, and I didn't want to be stuck sitting on the sidelines. I decided I'd rather just stay in the motel room that evening, but my parents wouldn't hear of it. After all, this was a weekend of celebrating, I was part of the family, and EVERYONE was going to the dance.

I grudgingly hobbled to the gymnasium with the rest of the crowd and tried to smile, though it was obviously forced. As we entered the gym, the blaring music reminded me that this was going to be a long, somewhat lackluster night. I slouched into the corner of a bleacher and looked as sour as I possibly could, especially since I was alone and no one was looking, or so I thought.

Then, out of the corner of my eye, I caught someone watching me. He was about my age, give or take a year, and he had thick hair and beautiful eyes. And he was in a wheelchair. Gingerly wheeling himself toward me, he flashed a set of perfect teeth.

He had a spark that seemed to ignite when he spoke, and he obviously enjoyed being surrounded by so much commotion and life. Before long, we were laughing and talking as though we had known each other forever.

Michael said that he used to be a great baseball player until multiple sclerosis set in at age 15. He slowly deteriorated, continually able to do less and less, and was now basically attached to his chair. But he focused on the positive, drawing strength in his ability to continue living in spite of his disability. Rather than referring to what he could not do, Michael focused on what he *could* do. Michael saw himself as a miracle and, even

I have never lost track of my life since that night. It was the night I learned how to dance, not with my body, but with my soul.

though he no longer played on a team, he could still toss a ball around or be a mentor to a less fortunate child. Even though he could not dance with his feet, he could sway to the music and dip his shoulders to the beat.

Michael was wheelchair-bound forever. He would not ever dance, or run, or walk for that matter. He would never use his feet again. But he was vibrant and alive and intelligent and interesting. He was dancing with his heart and soul.

I began to shrink in my shame and self-pity. How dare I feel sorry for what I could not do! My sprained ankle would pass—it was only a temporary condition.

Michael and I continued to talk and laugh, and I stopped looking longingly at the dancers on the gym floor stomping and swinging and swaying together. Instead, I began to look at them with joy and exuberance because I was now able to see the beauty of what the human body could do, even in a limited form.

Before the night was over, I was holding Michael's hand, and, together, we swayed gently to the music. We could dream that we were waltzing in Vienna or stomping at a Grateful Dead concert. I still tingle when I think of those moments we shared.

Michael gave me the profound gift of simply enjoying life—with no expectations, no demands, no projections, no strings.... I have never lost track of my life since that night. It was the night I learned how to dance, not with my body, but with my soul.

BY ELIZABETH TOOLE

WAYNE MESSMER
The Voice of Chicago

◈ ◈ ◈

C AN YOU IMAGINE a sports icon who's almost as beloved to Chicago as Michael Jordan or the late sports announcer Harry Caray? Sammy Sosa, you think? How about "Mr. Cub" himself, Ernie Banks? Would you believe Wayne Messmer? *"Who?"* you may ask.

Messmer, who's well known to the Chicago sports world as "Mr. Star-Spangled Banner," has sung the national anthem for White Sox, Cubs, Wolves, Blackhawks, and Bulls games. Fans have said that hearing Messmer helps them feel more patriotic. "There is no one who sings 'The Star-Spangled Banner' at hockey, soccer or baseball games with greater feeling than he does," Roy Leonard, a WGN radio personality, declared in an August 30, 1992, *Chicago Tribune* article.

Messmer has often been described as the "golden-throated baritone." He enjoys singing the musically challenging national anthem because it projects a wholesome family image, as he described in a *Tribune* interview. This is the image Messmer himself has projected, as a role model for kids, making personal appearances at youth groups and schools.

But in the early morning hours of April 9, 1994, hours after singing at a Blackhawks game, Messmer's "ideal" life changed forever.

A SHOT RINGS OUT

After leaving a Blackhawks gathering at Hawkeye's Bar and Grill on Taylor Street, Messmer was pulling away in his car when two teens approached him in a robbery attempt. One of them suddenly shot Messmer in the throat with a 9mm handgun, shattering the window. The teens fled, and Messmer drove himself back to the restaurant to get help. Someone spotted Messmer in his car and called an ambulance.

Due to Messmer's stature in the sports world, the shooting was covered with the attention normally given to a major celebrity. Daily news items were broadcast about his status. "I thought [the shooting] would be a small news item," Messmer said in a 1994 *Tribune* article. "I'm a guy who sings the anthem at hockey [games]…and reads the lineups here at Wrigley Field. What followed was unbelievable."

A multitude of letters wishing Messmer well came from all over the United States and Europe. If Messmer had not realized his popularity before then, this experience proved it. But how did all of the accolades begin?

A LIFE FILLED WITH MUSIC

Raised on Chicago's southwest side, Messmer attended Five Holy Martyrs Elementary School and then went to Kelly High School. Wayne got interested in music early on. He asked for an accordion at the age of eight and was soon mimicking tunes he'd heard on the Lawrence Welk and Mitch Miller shows.

In high school, he began playing the French horn and continued that in college. The voice work did not begin until his second year at Illinois Wesleyan University in Bloomington, Illinois. There Messmer majored in

"There is no one who sings 'The Star-Spangled Banner' at hockey, soccer or baseball games with greater feeling than he does."

the French horn and minored in voice. A fork in the road of his life appeared when he earned a spot in the Collegiate Choir.

One professor gave Messmer solos because of his "unusually good" voice. With that encouragement, Messmer and a friend from his music fraternity began performing at a local club for $35 a night.

After college, Messmer put down the French horn for good and took private voice lessons with voice teacher Melba Thrasher back in Chicago. He worked as a substitute teacher for a year, then taught general music at St. Turibius on Chicago's southwest side. He was also working toward a master's degree in guidance and counseling at Loyola University, which he received in 1974. Messmer was about to pursue a doctorate at Northwestern University when a stint on the radio changed the direction of his life.

BECOMING CHICAGO'S VOICE

Messmer got his feet wet by reading commercials on a German-language program, reporting the weather, and playing jazz records. Later, he became the sports director for WAGO. He was also a disc jockey for a national broadcast on Illinois's Saturday Music Network.

Messmer then moved to the better-known, widely broadcast station WLS as a midday newsman. Not one to be idle, Messmer was also a sports announcer for the Chicago Sting soccer team starting in 1980.

Through all of that, Messmer still managed to find time to sing at weddings, in clubs, and for the Chicago White Sox. He had been asked to do the public address announcements for the Sox at Comiskey Park, and he sang the national anthem for them during the 1982–84 seasons.

Because of his early morning radio commitments, Messmer decided to leave the Sox (often a late-night gig) and become a field announcer and

The future continued to look bright for Wayne Messmer until that fateful night in April 1994.

anthem singer for the Cubs, whose games were then played only during the day. His celebrity status gained him yet another role in 1991, as a New York Yankees announcer in the movie *The Babe.* That same year, he became vice president of marketing for Clearbrook Center, a not-for-profit center for developmentally disabled adults and children.

Messmer was never one to shy away from new ventures. A later career move landed him as executive vice president of the newest sports team to grace Chicago: the Wolves organization of the International Hockey League.

The future continued to look bright for Wayne Messmer until that fateful night in April 1994.

THE LONG JOURNEY BACK

Blackhawks players were as much in shock as Messmer when he arrived back at Hawkeye's Bar and Grill, the place he had left just minutes before. The 1:50 A.M. shooting led to ten hours of surgery at Cook County Hospital. Messmer's long road to recovery had begun.

The sports world was outraged at the attack. Grant Mulvey, the general manager of the Wolves, offered a $25,000 reward for anyone with information that could lead to the arrest and conviction of the shooter.

While Messmer recuperated, a tape of his voice singing the national anthem was played at a Blackhawks game. Still, "it's just not the same without Wayne," *Tribune* sports columnist Paul Sullivan lamented, quoting from a sign hanging at the old Chicago Stadium two days after the shooting.

During that time, Kathleen Messmer, herself a vocalist, made an appearance on behalf of her husband at the last Blackhawks game of the

1994 season—it was also the last game in the old Chicago Stadium. Messmer himself appeared at the Cubs Memorial Day game. Although he was not ready to sing just yet, fans were thrilled just to catch a glimpse of the man they cared so much about. Messmer went to the mound for the opening pitch, and everyone jumped to their feet.

Messmer wanted to sing for the Cubs during August, but he was sidelined by the baseball strike. He was also scheduled to sing at the Blackhawks' season opener on October 2, but the NHL lockout curtailed that. His comeback finally happened at the Chicago Wolves' debut game at the Rosemont Horizon on October 14, 1994. Since Messmer had helped bring this new team to life, it was especially fitting that he should make his comeback singing for them.

That Friday evening was described as magical, not because Chicago hockey fans were excited about the new team, nor because the Wolves beat the Detroit Vipers 4–2. No, the highlight of the evening was Messmer's singing of the national anthem, a triumph that no one would have missed. Until that Friday, Messmer had not sung before an audience since he'd been shot. When Wayne and Kathleen Messmer stepped out onto the ice, the crowd of 16,623 went wild.

Thanks to his own stubborn determination and the love and support of his wife and fans, Messmer was finally back where he belonged. "Dying was never an option," Messmer said in a May 1994 *Tribune* article. "Maybe it was my strong faith, my will, or maybe it was just plain stupidity. But, no, dying was never an option."

But what made Messmer's experience even more of a triumph can be traced back to the incident that brought him so close to death. You

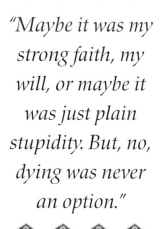

"Maybe it was my strong faith, my will, or maybe it was just plain stupidity. But, no, dying was never an option."

see, the shot that hit Messmer in the throat that April night had damaged his esophagus and larynx. Even if he did survive the shooting, no one had been sure if the "golden-throated" baritone would ever sing again. Had the bullet been only a half-inch over, this Chicago legend would have been silenced forever.

For many people, such an experience would make them fearful and bitter, but Messmer decided that forgiveness was the only path to true healing. In spring 1999, he went to the jails where his attackers are serving time so he could confront them face-to-face. He didn't want to just forgive them in his mind—he wanted the boys to know they were forgiven. Messmer is now writing a book about the entire shooting incident, so that others can learn from what he's been through.

Wayne Messmer has long been hailed as the "voice of Chicago." But now the beauty of his golden voice doesn't just come from his healed throat—it also comes from his mended heart.

BY LINDA WASHINGTON

WHY MISTI?

◆ ◆ ◆

HE CHAPLAIN PERFORMED the nuptial service before 300 guests, most of them in tears. "Today, we gather here to witness a miracle," he began.

The mother of the bride, Louise Ray Morningstar, watched her daughter, Misti—dressed in white satin, pearls, and lace—let go of her father's arm and take the hand of her groom. Louise's tears were more than tears of joy—they were tears of hope realized and years of uncertainty swept away.

Mothers of daughters dream, from the moment they know their baby is a girl, that one day that tiny armful of human potential will be a beautiful bride and a loving wife and mother, physically, emotionally, and spiritually ready to fulfill her own hopes and dreams.

For 17 years, nothing nibbled away at Louise's maternal assumptions. She watched the evening news from a detached distance, with its images of blood and twisted metal, microphones shoved into faces haloed by the neon lights of emergency rooms as if stunned "next of kin" could wrap words around the sudden death of their expectations. Louise knew that tragedy could strike as close as next door, but she never imagined tragedy striking one of her own children.

Her assumptions grew firmer as Misti bloomed. Her childhood love of rhythm matured into the dedicated study of ballet. Misti applied her genius IQ at a demanding boarding school to gain academic grounding and discipline for medical school and earn the credentials she needed to give back to a world that had given so much to her. Just looking at Misti, the grace of her stride, her beauty, assured Louise that this child was blessed. Nor was Misti's loveliness superficial. Her strong sense of personhood and her dignity quietly commanded respect, while the exuberance of her teenage years brought frequent smiles. She had best friends and good friends, and she knew the difference between them. She edited the yearbook, and she shopped with a passion. She had a boyfriend, Max, and in her closet hung a formal gown purchased months before her senior prom.

All that ended in a moment, beneath an 18-wheeler, where Misti lay crushed in the family car, which she had been driving to the mall. The truck driver walked away unharmed, stammering, "I never saw the intersection." Later, he paid a $40 traffic fine. Misti was taken away by helicopter. While a team of doctors fought to keep her lungs working and her heart beating, a nurse slipped a "Jane Doe" identification bracelet on her arm.

Louise and her husband, Harry, were in the Caribbean celebrating their new direction in life. After 35 years of marriage, two sons launched into adulthood, and Misti soon to enter college, they had sold their two businesses and decided to enjoy the good life. They would take trips, spend more time with friends and family, and enjoy the world's beauty in leisure. They watched the sunset over the ocean and had their last carefree conversation for five years.

It was just hours from that sunset to the high-tech life support systems surrounding Misti. In those hours a mother's questions changed

Her strong sense of personhood and her dignity quietly commanded respect, while the exuberance of her teenage years brought frequent smiles.

from "Where will Misti go to college?" to "Will Misti last the night?" to "Will she last the hour?"

After a month of many close calls with death, Misti's condition stabilized. She was in a coma, diagnosed with "brain trauma." Louise was warned not to expect further improvement in her daughter's quality of life. That day, she noticed another brain trauma patient making a great effort to propel his wheelchair. Inch by inch, the chair moved toward a spot of sun beneath a window. Louise realized that she had no assumptions left, only hope that the daughter who had wanted to be a doctor would one day be able to push her wheelchair to a sunny spot. Hope is what kept Louise fighting for every inch of progress that friends and family, doctors and therapists, and she herself could wrestle from her daughter's deep sleep. For a month they walked the tightrope between hope and dread. Now Misti was opening her eyes for short periods of time. Perhaps she was slowly reconnecting with the world, but no one knew what remained of the young woman she had been.

Through months of daylong visits in the rehabilitation hospital, Louise learned that coming out of a coma is not the gentle awakening Hollywood portrays. This is particularly true when the brain has been traumatized and all the circuits broken, bruised, or rearranged as Misti's were. She could sit in a wheelchair, but her muscles had not relearned their functions. Every limb, her torso, and her head had to be propped, strapped, restrained. Before she could learn to speak again, she had to learn to swallow, to move her lips, control her tongue. This 17-year-old honor student was in diapers; she wore bibs and she drooled. She made progress in regaining control of her body through intensive therapy and a mother who complained if she did not get every full session that was ordered. Louise learned the techniques and worked with her daughter, giving all the energy she could muster to the task of salvaging all of Misti that could be recovered.

Progress was slow but definite. Misti touched everything to learn how it felt, put everything in her mouth to learn how it tasted. Louise helped her daughter navigate a second infancy, but this time with no expectations of how far she would progress. Only hope remained that having beaten the odds by surviving, Misti would conquer the next hurdle. Louise did not dwell on any thoughts beyond that.

As she regained strength, sweet-natured Misti started to behave like a wild animal. She would lie very still, but when anyone got near, she would try to attack them, biting the nearest arm, hand, or leg. The doctor explained that she was fighting to get out of the coma, to make contact in any way possible. During this phase, her grandmother was able to visit her for the first time. She was shocked and grieved. "Why Misti?" she cried. After endless days and nights of her own heart asking "Why Misti?" Louise answered, "Why not Misti? Perhaps God felt we were more able to handle the devastating results of such an accident than some other parents."

Louise steeled herself for the next hurdle, which turned out to be a nightmare. In addition to reconnecting with the world through the use of her teeth, now Misti became an exhibitionist, stripping off her clothes and yelling swear words. The rehab team was pleased at the progress these actions represented. Louise focused on the word "progress" and trusted that her daughter would regain her dignity someday.

◆ ◆ ◆ ◆

"I have a hard time listening to people who take a 'poor me' stance to their lives. At the same time, I make more time for what's really important: my family, beauty, good friends."

◆ ◆ ◆ ◆

Months later, the rehab hospital discharged Misti to her family's care and prescribed a full schedule of physical, mental, and psychological therapy. At that time Misti was functioning intellectually at a fourth-grade level and had the emotional maturity of a three-year-old. Her emotional makeup was seriously damaged. She would laugh instead of cry. She was convinced that events she saw on television happened to her. Her fierce temper tantrums made her nearly impossible to control. Yet, Louise accepted the challenge of taking her daughter home less than a year after the accident. As they left the hospital, she heard a nurse say, "I don't know where that woman gets her guts, but if I ever get hurt, I want her on my side."

It would be four-and-a-half more years before Misti was fully launched back into life.

As a baby, Misti had not entered the strong and capable Morningstar family in the way you may have assumed. This child of the heart—reborn in adult life through a family's five years of labor, tears, exhaustion, and pain—was not expected, but selected. Misti had been adopted at ten weeks, though she was almost denied the opportunity to become a member of the family in which she went on to thrive. The system was against placing a healthy newborn with parents so near the arbitrary cutoff age who had two birth children of their own. But otherwise-healthy Misti had a "flaw" that opened a crack in the system and allowed her to be placed in Louise's arms: On each little foot, Misti had an extra toe.

From layette to bridal veil, Misti's life journey was not what her mother had imagined. The detour through brain trauma left lasting scars. Misti graduated from college, but medical school was out of the question.

Her emotions are unpredictable, and some tasks are difficult. Some may always be impossible. Regression is a possibility, but so is continued progress. Louise knows that lives are built on reality and not on assumptions. Holding Misti's son in her arms and knowing how dearly her son-in-law loves her daughter are miracles as well as the assurance she needs to know that Misti is fulfilling her destiny.

And so is Louise. She chronicled Misti's story in a book, *Journey Through Brain Trauma: A Mother's Story of Her Daughter's Recovery.* And five years after that carefree sunset over the ocean, Louise and her husband began their retirement again. "I'm not the person I was before the accident," she says. "I have a hard time listening to people who take a 'poor me' stance to their lives. At the same time, I make more time for what's really important: my family, beauty, good friends."

BY CAROL STIGGER

THE POWER OF DREAMS

◆ ◆ ◆

This is Bob Love's story of pride, determination, and ultimate triumph.

LONG BEFORE Michael Jordan took the Chicago Bulls to the summit of the NBA, there was another person in the history of the franchise who made his own mark in the record books. Loyal basketball fans across the country know of the man who scored an amazing 12,623 career points during his eight seasons with the Bulls. His name is Bob Love, and his story is one of exhilarating highs, debilitating lows, and constant faith in the power of dreams.

Bob grew up in rural Louisiana as one of 14 children. His family was extremely poor. And as if that wasn't enough, Bob struggled with something most of us take for granted: He had a stuttering problem and was unable to speak easily. The impediment was so debilitating that many times Bob would go for long periods without speaking at all. Other times, he stumbled his way awkwardly through conversations.

Bob escaped his disability and poverty through his dreams of becoming a basketball star. Despite the conditions and limited financial resources he had to live with, the determined young boy set his sights high and persevered. Unable to afford actual basketball equipment, Bob improvised by nailing a coat hanger to the side of his grandmother's house, using an imaginary ball to chase his dream.

Bob began to see his dream come true in his senior year of high school. He became the first player from Southern University to be named to the All-America team by the National Association of Intercollegiate

Athletics. Upon college graduation, he played for the Cincinnati Royals (now the Sacramento Kings), the Milwaukee Bucks, and then finished his career playing eight seasons with the Chicago Bulls.

Until Michael Jordan came along, Bob Love was the Chicago Bulls' catalyst and star. In addition to being the second-highest scorer in franchise history and being named to the All-Star team three times, Bob holds the Bulls playoff record for consecutive free throws in a game, going 17-for-17 against the Golden State Warriors in 1975. But despite his success on the basketball court, Bob said he heard over and over, "Bob Love is a stutterer. Bob Love can't talk." His inability to speak fluidly cost him numerous opportunities.

"Despite leading the team in 90 percent of the games I played in, I was never voted star of the game because of my speech problem," Bob explains. "They would put me on the bench the last two minutes of the game so I wouldn't be interviewed."

The three-time NBA All-Star was forced to retire from the Bulls in 1976 after he hurt his back. His days as a basketball star were over. Bob's wife left him, taking all of her possessions, explaining that she did not want to be married to "a stutterer and a cripple."

"Remember, back then pros didn't make that much money, and I needed to support my family," Bob explains. "I had an education, so I thought I should be able to get a job. But I was turned down time after time. People just wouldn't hire me after they heard me speak."

Bob continues, "To be a stutterer, or unable to communicate, can be one of the most devastating of disabilities. People think you are not as smart as you are. I was just as smart as anyone in my class, but because I couldn't talk, teachers looked at me differently." But Bob believed that one day he could overcome his disability. "I never stuttered in my dreams," he explains.

Bob struggled to find work for several years because of his speech impediment. Then, in 1984, the former NBA All-Star took a job at Nordstrom in Seattle, Washington, busing tables and washing dishes for $4.45 an hour. It became the most humiliating and embarrassing time of his life. Former players and their children would see him cleaning tables, and Bob would overhear people whisper things like, "Hey, that's Bob Love… used to be a great basketball player…what a shame."

Most people would probably wither under such detrimental comments, but those words only made Bob stronger. He made up his mind that if he had to be a dishwasher, he "would become the best dishwasher in the world." Bob continued working in this position for more than a year, trying to keep a positive outlook.

Then, one day, the owners of Nordstrom commented on what a great job Bob was doing. They told him they wanted to promote him but felt they couldn't unless he got help for his stuttering. Best of all, they offered to pay for his speech training. After so many years of humiliation and embarrassment, Bob Love, at age 45, was going to become a new man.

He went for therapy with Susan Hamilton of University Way Speech Services in Seattle. "I had to start over learning to talk," Bob remembers. "As I progressed, Susan helped me learn to speak in more and more difficult situations. But she always went with me and stood behind me. If I got hung up, we would go back to the office and she would help me through the problem."

Bob's first speech was at a high school banquet in front of 700 people. To him, it looked like a million. "I struggled through every moment, but I did it. Once I was through, those people stood up and gave me a standing ovation. It was the greatest moment of my life," Bob recalls with tremendous pride. He says the ovation surpassed anything he did playing basketball because it was done in appreciation of the tremendous personal growth he had made. "Now I knew I could speak in front of people, and there would be no stopping me!" Bob says proudly.

As the Bulls were beginning to build their dynasty, Bob received a call in 1992 from Steve Schanwald, the Bulls vice president of marketing and broadcasting, asking if he'd be interested in a position with the team. The Chicago fans still loved him, and they wanted him to come back. Bob was offered the position of director of community relations, and he promptly accepted. He dropped to his knees and gave thanks to God for his blessings.

But that wasn't the only good fortune that came into Bob's life after his long series of troubling setbacks. The Bulls retired his famous number 10 jersey before a sellout crowd at Chicago Stadium on January 14, 1994. Then, on December 8, 1995, Bob married Rachel Dixon at a ceremony during halftime of a Chicago Bulls–San Antonio Spurs game. As his life turned around, Bob continued speaking out about how his disability had changed his life for the better. In addition to his community relations work with the Bulls, Bob is also a motivational speaker who talks to approximately 350,000 kids every year all across the country.

◈ ◈ ◈ ◈

Bob believed that one day he could overcome his disability. "I never stuttered in my dreams," he explains.

◈ ◈ ◈ ◈

"I emphasize to students that they have two choices in life: to succeed, and to succeed again.... Anything they will do or accomplish all begins with a dream, and they should never let anyone tell them they can't accomplish their dream," he says encouragingly. "Without my disability, I would not be the person I am or have the life I have. It made me better."

Many people want today's athletic stars to serve as role models, but, unfortunately, many of those athletes aren't up to the challenge. The perils faced by Bob Love during his life and the courage and determination with which he dealt with them make him a role model of the highest order. He never made a lot of money. He turned negatives into positives. He always tried his hardest, no matter what he was doing, and he never lost sight of his dreams. Bob sums it up when he says, "Don't give up and always try to do your best. If you take the first step, someone will help you take the next one."

BY **RICH BRIGGS**

BLESSINGS IN DISGUISE

◆ ◆ ◆

*L*IFE IS OFTEN FILLED with tragedy. But I've learned that every tragedy has the potential to become a blessing. Sometimes we have to look through the thick, dark clouds of life to see the extraordinary rainbow of colors in the sky.

I learned how to look for the rainbows at the tender age of nine, through the help of a very special friend. My lesson began one hazy, humid August day. The high school was playing their first football game of the season, and my sister, a trumpet player, was scheduled to march with the band at the halftime show. My brother asked me if I wanted to go to the game. I really didn't feel like going, but I said yes anyway. After all, he rarely asked me to do anything with him.

As my brother, his friends, and I eagerly climbed into the car, we had no idea what kind of a storm was beginning to brew.

On our way to the game, we sang and chattered excitedly as we drove down the highway. Then, suddenly, everything changed. I'm not exactly sure what happened next—I woke up two days later in a hospital bed. My mother told me that we had been in a horrible car accident, and the other children were also hurt. But she said we all would soon recover. I turned to look at my brother, who was lying in the bed next to mine. I could hardly recognize him! His face was swollen and badly bruised.

"Ronnie, are you okay?" I asked. He slowly nodded his head. I was relieved, but I was also in terrible pain.

◆ ◆ ◆ ◆

Although my childhood car accident was a horrible, frightening experience, it provided some unexpected blessings in disguise.

◆ ◆ ◆ ◆

"Mommy, my back hurts," I said, trying to hold back the tears. "I know honey," she said soothingly. "You have a few broken bones, but you're going to be okay."

Later that evening, a doctor came into my room and told me I had four broken bones in my back and one in my neck. He said I was going to be transported to another hospital where I'd receive a full-length body cast. Fear and sadness washed over me in an uncontrollable wave. I was already homesick, and I didn't want to leave my brother's side.

Upon my arrival at the new hospital, a doctor approached me with a wheelchair. Due to the nature of my injuries, I would have to use the wheelchair until the cast could be applied later in the week. My mother had to leave for a while, and as she kissed me good-bye, I was again overwhelmed by fear and sadness.

A short time later, my mother returned with a nurse, who directed us to a playroom at the other end of the hall. Inside the room, a woman sat next to a little girl. They were making signals with their hands. This little girl looked very strange to me. She had no hair, wore thick, dark glasses, and half of her face sagged sadly toward her shoulder. I wondered what they were doing with their hands. The woman turned to me and smiled. She said they were talking to each other in sign language, and the little girl wanted to play with me.

For the rest of the week, this woman served as our translator. Every day, my new friend and I would meet in the playroom to talk, play, and laugh for hours. My initial curiosity about her appearance was quickly replaced by my eagerness to have fun playing together.

The day before I was scheduled to receive my cast, I rolled down to the playroom, but the little girl was gone. Our translator told me that my playmate was having surgery that morning to remove a tumor from her brain. My mother quietly took me back to my room.

The next day, the doctors came to take me downstairs where they would apply the cast. I didn't care about the cast anymore. All I wanted was to find out if my new friend was okay. I knew that I would be going home soon, and I wanted to tell her good-bye. Unfortunately, I wasn't able to see her or find out how she was doing. Even so, her courage, inner joy, and friendship changed my life forever.

Many years have passed, and I have fully recovered. I developed a love for working with children, so I went to college and became a teacher. I decided to take a sign language class, and on the first day I realized I already knew one word. I knew the sign that means "friend."

I now teach at a preschool, and I especially love working with children who have special needs. My goal is to show the other children that those who look or act different from them are not "weird." Children with special needs can smile, talk, play, laugh, and even become friends.

Although my childhood car accident was a horrible, frightening experience, it provided some unexpected blessings in disguise. I often wonder if I would have become a preschool teacher if I hadn't befriended that odd-looking little girl in the hospital. She's the one who taught me to see past the dark clouds of life and always look for the rainbows.

BY **RENAY JUSTICE**

◆ ◆ ◆ ◆

I decided to take a sign language class, and on the first day I realized I already knew one word. I knew the sign that means "friend."

◆ ◆ ◆ ◆

KAREN DUFFY'S TRUE BEAUTY

❖ ❖ ❖

*A*T WAS SEPTEMBER 1995, and I was doing really well. I had finished my stint as an MTV veejay and landed small parts in the movies *Reality Bites* and *Dumb & Dumber.* At 33, I was a spokesperson for Revlon's Charlie perfume, and the show I was working on as a correspondent, Michael Moore's *TV Nation*, had been nominated for an Emmy for best information series. I went to the Emmys as George Clooney's date—we're old pals, and he'd also been nominated. My show won, but, unfortunately, a terrible headache tainted the night.

The next morning it got worse—to the point that I knew something was wrong. I flew home to New York, called my doctor, and went to see him right from the airport. He examined me and immediately sent me for an MRI. I was joking and chatting with the technician, and all of a sudden she wouldn't even look at me. She just said, "Call your doctor."

What they found was a lesion in my brain—technically it's called a C7—and it was already several inches long. As it grew it did a tremendous amount of nerve damage. They didn't know whether it was multiple sclerosis or something called sarcoidosis (an incurable inflammatory disease of unknown origin); since sarcoidosis is so rare, they figured the chances of that were impossible. Within two days they diagnosed me with MS just because I fit the profile. It took about ten months before I got a definitive diagnosis, so from September 1995 until

June 1996, I was just making wills and preparing to die. There were weeks when I couldn't move; I was literally paralyzed. Feeding myself was impossible because I couldn't hold a fork, and I was bedridden for about three months that winter. There were times when I'd get a little better and get booted up on steroids, and then I'd work. But the steroids distorted my face—steroids redeposit fat where you didn't have it before. So I would get a big round puffy face and eyelids, which changed my looks entirely. It was weird because during my illness, Revlon gave me the entire Almay campaign. The Almay tag line is "Stay healthy, stay looking your best." I kept thinking, "Yeah, I wish I could."

During this time, I didn't tell anyone I was sick. My agent told me not to; she said no one would hire me because they wouldn't be able to put out an insurance rider on me. I felt bad because it was like trying to keep a beach ball under water. I didn't lie, exactly. We just said I had a neurological problem of unknown origin.

The first time I went out (after I got sick) was around Christmas. My boyfriend took me to the movies and got me some hot tea. I had a seizure and threw tea all over the people around me. After we broke up, a friend of mine wanted to fix me up with her friend, Richard, so she invited me for dinner. One of my girlfriends came over and put some eyeliner on me—I couldn't put on makeup and my hair was falling out, but I was still up for dating! I showed up at the house, and her friend Richard turned out to be Richard Gere! I had my hand in a sling because I couldn't hold a fork, so he cut all my food for me and fed me. In the middle of dinner, I had a seizure, knocked over the centerpiece, and set the table on fire. Richard put it out. I just laughed because there was nothing else I could

Having sarcoidosis has shown me that I used to live life the way some people drive a rental car—hitting the gas, taking the turns. I was happy to begin with, but this illness has made me much more engaged.

do. He made me feel comfortable, though. He was so cute. I just said I had a weird neurological thing and I didn't know what was going on. To this day, he still calls to see how I'm doing.

Initially, I was overwhelmed with shame about my disability—which wasn't logical. That was really hard. Only my family and my close friends knew about my illness. My mom and my best friends and even my agent would come and take care of me. My brother would sit with me and watch TV, and I'd be on the phone with my two sisters every day. I even had doormen who took care of me. It was hard for me to accept a lot of help, but it's amazing how much love and support is out there, if you allow yourself to accept it.

I didn't look the same, and working on TV as a reporter and a representative for a beauty company was difficult. In March 1996, I was invited to the Academy Awards—I was working for Revlon, and they sponsored the Oscars. *Entertainment Tonight* wanted to film me and the other Revlon spokespersons, Daisy Fuentes and Claudia Schiffer, getting ready. It was my first television appearance in eight months. My girlfriend from MTV was doing my makeup, but I didn't know the hairstylist, so I pulled her aside and said, "Listen, I'm going through a really weird medical thing and my hair's falling out, so just put a pin in it and I'll put a hat on." She was great—she said, "No problem, I'll take care of it." But as soon as we did it, one of the pins fell out with all this hair in it, and the manicurist screamed, "Oh my gosh! All your hair's falling out!" The cameras were rolling, but they had the generosity not to air it. The woman didn't know how devastating that was for me. I remember calling my mother and crying.

When I finally came clean, things got so much easier. I had to accept that this was going to be part of my life forever. Without a firm diagnosis I had the luxury of hoping for the best. But once they knew it was sarcoidosis, then I had to come to terms with it.

After I was properly diagnosed, I was in the hospital for a couple weeks. I was so sick, they really didn't think I was going to make it. They even gave me last rites. I was in such incredible agony. I have a tremendous amount of nerve damage in my brain and my central nervous system, because as these lesions grow they destroy everything. I always have pain in my hands, neck, and shoulders. I can't be touched from the top of my head to the middle of my chest, which makes putting on clothes really hard. It's a sharp, burning, stinging pain that spikes every 10 or 15 seconds. It has never stopped; we're just controlling it with medication, which is such a blessing.

I knew from the minute I got this headache that my life would never be the same. I'm pretty tough, but this was such a different realm of intense pain, it just didn't seem like people could live for long like this. That's what I was imagining, anyway. But somehow I pulled through and managed to get a little better.

The summer after the diagnosis I was hired as a correspondent on a television show called *American Journal*, but I was too sick to do it. By that point, I couldn't even hold a microphone steady, and they wanted me to travel, which was impossible. But I was afraid of not being able to earn a living—my medical bills were astounding, and my insurance didn't cover everything. I was still signed to Revlon, but I figured, "Who's going to keep me on?" You know, there isn't a big market for bald-headed,

It was hard for me to accept a lot of help, but it's amazing how much love and support is out there, if you allow yourself to accept it.

steroid-bloated models, so I didn't think that would be a possibility. I was the Charlie Girl, and that's about youth and vitality—it's not about brain tumors and chemotherapy.

What's interesting is that after I realized I couldn't do the reporting, I started writing, which is something I had always wanted to do. At the time, I couldn't even hold a pencil. I would write as much as I could, and then my brother—a newspaper editor—typed it into a computer and edited it for me. The nerve damage got so bad that I lost all the feeling in both hands, both feet, and my neck, but I always had my index and middle fingers. I can eat and write now, but I still can't type. I lost something, but I found this—I found writing. And I lost the ability to travel—I had traveled all over the world, to Europe, Asia, Australia—but I found John Lambrose, the man I love more than anything, and he lived right next door to me.

The day I got out of the hospital in June 1996, my friends picked me up, and we drove straight to their summer house. John was visiting there, too. I spent a lot of the summer just recuperating, but the steroids were making me feel really confused and in the depths of despair. Nevertheless, I was happy not to be in the hospital.

So I was at my worst that summer and fall—bloated and not exactly Miss Congeniality—and John fell in love with me anyway. He is really kind. We started dating that autumn when we got back to Manhattan. I've always had such incredible admiration for him. He's perfect. He's really smart, and he's just so cute. I love everything about him.

At first I told John, "I think we should throw this on ice. Let's wait until I get better and then get back to it." And he said, "Absolutely not.

I've fallen in love with a woman who's got a lump in her head. Big deal."
I was very emphatic about him realizing exactly what he was getting into
because I felt it was the fair thing to do. I didn't want to scare him away,
but I really wanted to be honest. I didn't want to hurt him by not being
able to be his partner.

In January 1997, we were lying on the couch watching a movie and he
said, "Let's run away." I said, "I'm 36 years old, what am I going to run
away from?" He said, "Let's run away and get married." So we got married
in Jamaica on the last day of February 1997.

It's been great. I am so blessed to have him in my life. Just the other
day, I was wondering if our relationship is so peaceful because I have a
disease that's incurable, or if it's because I've never been in love like this
(which I think is true). We really have an amazing respect for each other.
There are so many things I love about him. We have a normal relationship
in which there are ups and downs, but we just don't hang onto things.

One thing I've noticed is that I'm much slower to anger now. I've
become much more compassionate. I don't know if it's from age or
enlightenment. I never know when I'm going to get sick again and not
be able to walk or eat pancakes or hold a fork or write, so it's made the
dimension of joy in my life just explode. It definitely makes me much
more understanding.

I don't think of myself as a sick person. I kind of forget about it, and
I think that's good. I was talking to my doctor and I said, "I live in denial."
And she said, "Of course you do. If you didn't, it would be too hard."
She's right. So I'm always thinking positively. When I go into the hospi-
tal, I try to enjoy it. It's become something I don't dread. I like going

◆　◆　◆　◆

*I haven't really
been praying,
"Oh, heal me."
Maybe that'll
come, but right
now I just want to
be strong enough
to deal with it.*

◆　◆　◆　◆

there, I like the people, and I feel lucky that they're in my life. It's not such a terrible thing. These days, I'm off steroids, though I still go in for chemo once a week. It's a powerful drug, and it wipes me out. Later I feel like a train wreck, and I usually have a big stomachache the next day. But I just kind of fit it in with my day. It doesn't bother me that much.

It's amazing how strong you can be if you really want to do something. I had a small part in Woody Allen's movie, *Celebrity*. And I was in a movie with Rosie Perez called *The 24 Hour Woman*, which premiered at the Sundance Film Festival in January 1999. I played a talk-show host. They were both a lot of fun, and nobody treated me like I was sick.

My colleagues have been really great. Michael Nesmith told me, "Some people are insecure, some people wet the bed until they're 25. You've got a lump in your head. Big deal." And Michael Moore told me, "Everybody's got something. At least you know what yours is." Really, when you think like that, it makes you say, "Oh, it's no big deal."

Having sarcoidosis has shown me that I used to live life the way some people drive a rental car—hitting the gas, taking the turns. I was happy to begin with, but this illness has made me much more engaged. I'm not so distracted—it has definitely heightened my awareness. It's changed me in a lot of ways. For instance, I don't think I would have married and settled down before. I was just spinning. I had a lot of superfluous energy and movement, and now I'm a lot more focused. I have a plan and a goal. And, actually, getting better is not the first goal. Usually I pray to have the strength to handle this—that's always my first prayer. I haven't really been praying, "Oh, heal me." Maybe that'll come, but right now I just want to be strong enough to deal with it.

❖ ❖ ❖ ❖

"Some people are insecure, some people wet the bed until they're 25. You've got a lump in your head. Big deal."

❖ ❖ ❖ ❖

Sometimes I do pray to be pain-free—just for one minute. It never stops. There are times, usually in the evening, when I try not to take anything because, even though I've been taking morphine for three years, I'm always thinking, "Maybe tonight I'll be better and won't need it." I've never been better yet, but I'm always optimistic.

God gave me a gift as a communicator, and I thought it would be the height of hypocrisy if I didn't reveal the truth about my condition. And because I happen to have this modeling gig and do movies, I feel like I have an opportunity to demystify a lot of scary things. I talk to doctors at Sloan Kettering about what it's like to be a patient, and I also talk to patients. I work with the Comprehensive Epilepsy Center, and I talk to kids who are sick and going through seizures about how to deal with it.

Having a disease that doesn't have a cure has taught me a lot of valuable lessons—I've learned that I have a finite amount of time, so it's up to me to choose what's most valuable and what has meaning, and that has been very illuminating. So I'm only going to do things that I think are important and honorable.

As a therapist—I studied recreational therapy at the University of Boulder before I was "discovered"—I've been working with people with disabilities, and I've been a huge proponent politically for getting people with disabilities into the mainstream of our society.

If I didn't stand with honesty, I would be the biggest knucklehead. Everything I worked for would go down the drain if I couldn't live by what I believe. So that has changed me a lot. And it's cool.

BY KAREN DUFFY, AS TOLD TO LAUREN DAVID PEDEN

WAYNE ROSS
How the Ride of a Lifetime Changed His Life

◈ ◈ ◈

◈ ◈ ◈ ◈

"Biking was pretty much my life for many years, and this was going to be my opportunity to set a world record in cycling."

◈ ◈ ◈ ◈

T HE INTERESTING thing about Wayne Ross is that he says he's "keeping his fingers crossed."

It's a phrase that many of us hear often and probably don't think twice about. But what makes these words so remarkable is that the 33-year-old Ross, a contender for a world bicycling record just three years ago, can no longer move his fingers, his hands, or any other part of his body from his chest down.

Whether it's considered a cruel twist of fate or the will of God, when we're forced to deal with what seems an unfair turn of events in our lives, what matters most is how we deal with it. Wayne Ross has made that clear.

A RECORD-SETTING RIDE

It was a fluke that Ross participated at all on the bike ride that started in Alaska, 250 miles north of the Arctic Circle, and ended at the other end of the earth, at the tip of South America. Spike Ramsden, Ross's high school buddy from Scituate, Massachusetts, had been planning the bike journey with another partner. The almost-16,000-mile trip would also serve as a fund-raiser for the Multiple Sclerosis Foundation. But a month before the ride, Ramsden's partner dropped out, so Ramsden called upon Ross.

"Biking was pretty much my life for many years, and this was going to be my opportunity to set a world record in cycling," Ross said. "This was going to be my avenue into [the] Guinness [Book of World Records]."

Taking on big physical challenges was nothing new for Ross. At the age of six, he soloed a six-mile bike ride. As he grew older, Ross competed in marathons, biathlons, and triathlons, and he completed a bike trek across the United States. He also served three years in the U.S. Air Force before deciding to make biking his life by working for several cycle touring companies and doing odd jobs between paychecks.

Ross and Ramsden kicked off their trek on June 12, 1996, in the tundra at Prudhoe Bay. Their goal was to hit Argentina's Beagle Channel in nine months. Ten years earlier, a bike group had made the same trip, completing it in ten months and nine days.

With 100 pounds of gear each, Ross and Ramsden maneuvered through the cold, ice, and snow of Alaska before they hit better roads in The Yukon, British Columbia, Washington, and Oregon. Making good time with an average of 100 miles a day, Ross and Ramsden whizzed down the Pacific Coast through California and down into the Baja Coast of Mexico. Temperatures of 115 degrees and then the wrath of Hurricane Hernan got in their way, but their determination was fierce, and they soon reached Guatemala, the halfway point.

The two friends couldn't have been happier. They were actually ahead of schedule, and they spent the next four days in Guatemala City servicing their bikes and speaking about the Multiple Sclerosis Foundation to the media. They were even greeted by President Alvaro Arzu, with whom they dined the night before they set out on the second leg of their trip. Refreshed and primed to make their goal, Ross and Ramsden said good-bye to a crowd of well-wishers on October 23 and began their trip down a steep road out of Guatemala City.

Within a Split Second...

It's funny how a person retains seemingly insignificant details when things go horribly wrong. For Ross, it was the round Mercedes logo attached to the red van that suddenly stopped in the middle of the highway. He had glanced down to check his gears, and when he looked up the metal logo was rushing toward him. Ross's bike slammed into the van, forcing his head to "jam down into" his body. The impact threw Ross backward onto the road, and the excruciating pain was like "a red-hot poker in the neck." He felt nothing else in the rest of his body.

Ramsden, who was down the road by this time, immediately returned to Ross's side and took charge. Ross was rushed to a hospital in Guatemala City for emergency surgery. He had suffered a C 4–6 spinal injury, which meant that he'd shattered his fourth, fifth, and sixth vertebrae—just inches down from where the head and neck meet. Also, Ross's sixth vertebra had dislocated the seventh.

Most people who break their fourth vertebra are unable to breathe on their own, according to Ross, but somehow he was able to gasp shallow, labored breaths. "If I had been just a little worse off, I wouldn't have made it," he said, explaining that the first Guatemalan hospital he was taken to did not have a ventilator.

Once he was stabilized at a second, more advanced, Guatemalan hospital, Ross was airlifted—three days after the accident—back home to Massachusetts to the Boston Medical Center. Before Ross left Central America, Ramsden told him he would end the bike trip to fly back with him. Ross, however, persuaded Ramsden to complete the trek. Ramsden, now alone, finished the cross-continent journey in Ushuaia, Argentina, on March 3, 1997—just nine days short of nine months. He had broken the world record!

New Challenges, New Goals

For Ross, of course, his new challenges of enduring pain and embarking on a long, grueling rehabilitation process were just beginning. He was immobile from his chest down, unable to move his arms, and his emotional response to the accident was still raw. During the first ten weeks, Ross said he'd have the same nightmare: He would scream for Ramsden and then wake up thinking his injuries were just "a bad dream." Ross consciously realized the severity of his injuries, but said it "took awhile to set in."

Shortly after arriving in Boston, Ross told himself that before leaving the hospital, he would be able to not only raise his arms, but also pick himself up. Ross's condition improved steadily, and he was discharged four months later, but he couldn't yet lift himself. Ross was discouraged, but he didn't give up. Living at home with his parents and going to rehab every day, Ross continued to focus on strengthening his arms by working out on special weight machines. Little by little, he was able to raise his arms. And although he could not move his hands or fingers (he still cannot move them today), Ross was gaining movement in his wrists, allowing him to propel his wheelchair. He was also learning how to pick up a book, feed himself, and brush his teeth.

Then, 15 months after the accident, Ross experienced a momentous victory. He was finally strong enough to lift himself up! Now he would be able to get himself in and out of his wheelchair, a true delight for anyone who has lost most of his or her physical independence.

Fifteen months after the accident, Ross experienced a momentous victory. He was finally strong enough to lift himself up!

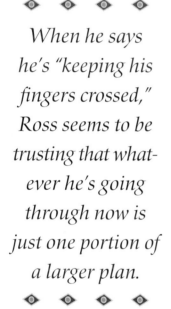

When he says he's "keeping his fingers crossed," Ross seems to be trusting that whatever he's going through now is just one portion of a larger plan.

But Ross's use of his arms and his increasing outer-body strength were just part of his amazing recovery. The accident left him with the ability to use only the top 10 percent of his lungs, causing him to force air down into the other 90 percent that is paralyzed. Breathing is "real shallow and it's impossible to take a deep breath," Ross says, but he has learned to be patient and relax.

Swimming has been an integral part of Ross's rehabilitation. Now capable of using the "full range of motion" of his arms, Ross is in the pool three to four times a week. An active swimmer before he broke his neck, Ross glides through the water unassisted, dragging his torso and legs. He entered a league made up of physically challenged people, and in 1997, Ross broke his league category's national record for the 200-meter backstroke. Scuba is something else Ross decided to resume. He had obtained an instructor's license in 1983 and is proud that he's now "diving with a broken neck," even in the ocean.

Despite reaching so many milestones in a relatively short time, Ross says he still has his bad days. For one thing, even though he can't move his hands, they are in constant pain. "They never not hurt all day, every day," he says. "They feel like they're in a vice." But the mental anguish of his limitations is worse. "Mentally, it still takes time.... It still bothers me a lot," he admits.

But there is an amazing well of hope at Ross's core. When he says he's "keeping his fingers crossed," Ross seems to be trusting that whatever he's going through now is just one portion of a larger plan. Ross frequently speaks of a "guardian angel" who not only looked after him right after the accident, but during the whole bike trip, and his belief in a higher being seems to give him a genuine sense of peace. After hitting the van and lying on the highway, Ross says he "never felt that anything was going to be that disastrously bad. I'm really hoping for a cure for spinal cord injuries. I'm very optimistic."

Ross has decided to focus his energies not just on his own recovery, but also on educating and inspiring others. He has already spoken to a number of business, school, and church groups and hopes to tell his story to many more people. His presentations cover a wide array of issues, including goal-setting, quadriplegia, physical fitness, education, geography, and bicycle safety.

Without the steadfast support of his family (his three sisters live nearby), friends, and even strangers, Ross says he would not be where he is today. Before the accident, Ross recalls, "I was very independent, and I had a loose relationship with my family." But now, he says, "I've become very dependent on my family and other people," and adds that he gets "choked up" when he thinks about all the help he's received. "I really never felt I did much to help people. I never expected to be on the receiving end," he says. "But whatever I did, I'm getting it back ten times."

BY SUSAN MORAN

THE LION AND THE MARATHON

❖ ❖ ❖

OR OUR FAMILY, March 1998 came in like a lion: a man-eater of a beast who attacked my husband without warning and threatened to take his life or, at least, leave it in shreds.

On the first Wednesday of that month, my husband, Witek Krajewski, woke up with a sharp pain in his back. He could hardly get up, and breathing was painful. I wondered if he'd pulled a muscle playing basketball the day before. At 44, my husband loved sports. His weekly schedule included coaching judo (he'd earned his black belt in Poland as a teenager), playing soccer (outdoors, all year, even in Iowa!), basketball, and jogging. He was probably involved in too many sports, he conceded, but that was what he needed to stay healthy and to counteract the pressures of a demanding job. He was proud of his low blood pressure and slow heart rate and the fact that, at his last physical exam, several doctors had gathered to admire the results of his stress EKG.

He left for work that morning still uncomfortable after trying a cold pack and some ibuprofen. That afternoon he called me, and I could hear from his labored breathing that he was in a lot of pain.

I took him to the doctor, who, with a cursory exam, diagnosed a pulled muscle. Probably, he suggested, from sitting at the computer for several hours the night before. We both frowned—that was not unusual. I asked the doctor about the painful breathing and whether he was going to listen to my husband's lungs. The doctor shrugged and said, "Only if you want me to." Surprised, I didn't insist. The doctor gave him a muscle relaxant.

Within hours, Witek's temperature rose alarmingly, he began to shake, his pain grew worse, and he seemed disoriented. As I tried to reach the doctor, I wished I would have insisted that he listen to Witek's lungs. I thought it might be pleurisy, an infection in the lining of the lungs. But the doctor on call thought he probably had a virus in addition to the pulled muscle her colleague had diagnosed, and she had me increase the pain medication. Over the next day and a half, Witek didn't improve, and a different muscle relaxant was prescribed. By then, he could barely sit up. The news was on, and I happened to hear about an outbreak of strep in Texas and Illinois that was killing people. I didn't think Witek had it, but I decided to take him to the emergency room.

The ER doctors could tell he was really sick. Blood tests indicated an infection, although it would be days before the specific bacteria could be identified. Witek was admitted to the hospital, put on IV antibiotics, and given something for pain. He grew sicker, and his case was turned over to an internist, who put him on morphine and ordered more tests. Within another day the grim diagnosis came back: invasive Strep A. Witek also had rapidly increasing congestion in his lungs and damage to his heart.

A thousand times deadlier than the bacteria that causes a strep throat, invasive strep is a blood-borne infection that attacks the patient's internal organs, especially the heart, which pumps the blood. This strain of strep is related to the infamous flesh-eating bacteria, but it destroys from the inside out.

The internist told me that Witek would be put on oxygen, switched immediately to penicillin—an antibiotic more effective against strep—and moved to the intensive care unit (ICU). She warned me that the situation was grave.

In the intensive care unit, two nurses huddled together over my husband's chart, peering at him sympathetically and shaking their heads. Our internist informed me that we should transfer Witek to the nearby University of Iowa Hospitals and Clinics, one of the Midwest's top medical centers. He needed the higher level of care provided there.

Outside, the wind chill was below zero. "Make sure he's covered up," I begged the ambulance attendants.

With our closest family more than 900 miles away, I called friends to help the children after school and take care of the animals.

Scores of doctors and assistants visited my husband's small cubicle in the University Hospital's ICU, and he was connected to a variety of monitors. The senior physician called me aside.

"I'm sure you realize how serious the situation is," he said. "Your husband's chances at this point are 50/50. How he does tonight will tell us whether he will survive."

I couldn't believe what he was saying.

"Oh yes," he said, emphatically, "this disease is a killer. It's very, very virulent." If the congestion in my husband's lungs grew any worse, he would have to be put on a respirator. "Unfortunately," the doctor said, "only 70 percent of people who go on respirators make it off."

By now, I was in shock.

I mumbled something about my husband's parents living in Poland. He suggested that if they could, they should come right away.

"You go home now," he said. "Even if things get worse, we still have several days."

I did go home, filled with dread, and found a message on the answering machine from Sheila Cannon, the mother of one of my children's friends. "Don't worry, we're praying for him," Sheila said. She went on to say she'd given Witek's name to a prayer group, Silent Unity, who held 24-hour prayer vigils. They would pray for him for 30 days. She hoped I didn't think this was too strange, but she firmly believed it would help. Like most people, I, too, often let the stress of daily life keep me from praying or meditating. But now, concerned only with my husband's life, I could see that spiritual help—prayer—was all there was. I was grateful to Sheila and to the unknown network of people who were at that moment praying for my husband. I joined with them fervently.

My mother called from 2,000 miles away and offered to telephone family and friends. "If people want to know what they can do to help, I'll ask them to pray. I'll hold him in the light."

I tried to do this, too, as I collapsed, exhausted, into bed. When I called the hospital early the next morning, they said he had not gotten worse. My heart leaped—wonderful news!

That morning Witek tried to smile. That afternoon they moved him to a step-down intensive care unit where they would continue to monitor him carefully. He had turned the corner and would slowly begin to regain his strength. But, the doctors cautioned, he had some damage to

Concerned only with my husband's life, I could see that spiritual help— prayer—was all there was.

his heart, although they didn't know how much. In any case, his recovery would take a long time.

That night I went home tired but heartened and found more than 15 messages from friends and family with offers of help ranging from child care to prayers. When I fell into bed it was with deep gratitude to the Almighty and to the network of friends and family—even people we didn't know—who were sending us their prayers and help.

Over the next few days, doctors conducted tests to determine how much damage Witek's heart had sustained. Incredibly, surprisingly, the valve that had been "full of vegetation" in the earlier X ray was now clear. Though he was still very sick, Witek had miraculously escaped permanent damage to his heart or any other organs. That day, especially, my prayers were full of thanks.

Witek could barely stand for his first walk a few days later, needing both me and a railing for support. His first steps on the road to recovery were unsteady ones down the hospital corridor.

Our doctors were right that it would be a long recovery. Because this infection was so invasive and virulent, Witek would have to continue the intravenous antibiotic for at least another month at home. This would be done through a "pic-line," a plastic tube installed in a vein that ran from just below his elbow, through his shoulder and chest, to a spot right above the heart. Someone would have to inject the antibiotic into this tube daily. To save the insurance company's money, I was elected, and was trained and initially supervised by a helpful staff of visiting nurses. I actually got quite good at it, but it was an awesome responsibility, and I worried obsessively about germs.

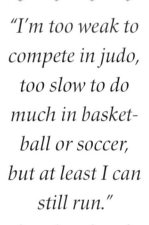

"I'm too weak to compete in judo, too slow to do much in basketball or soccer, but at least I can still run."

Witek's mother came from Warsaw to help. Fortunately, she enjoyed all sorts of weather, so she began to accompany her son on daily walks. At first these walks were short and slow: halfway to the barn the first day, all the way to the barn the next, then a short way down the road. They went a bit farther each day, until at the end of the month they walked to a sandwich shop two miles away. Then the pic-line was removed, his mother returned to Poland, and Witek began to jog, slowly, with the children. Keeping up with the kids was a challenge—at first.

After he returned to work full time, Witek told me he'd always planned to run a marathon once in his life, and he was thinking of doing it that fall.

"A marathon? Twenty-six miles? You're nuts!" I said.

"There's one in Chicago in October," he replied. "That gives me four months to train." He held up his hand to stop my protest. "I'm too weak to compete in judo, too slow to do much in basketball or soccer, but at least I can still run."

He developed a training schedule, stuck to it all summer, and by September he'd completed two 20-mile runs. It wasn't easy, he confided, and he wasn't sure he'd be able to run 26 miles.

"But if I don't finish, I'll have to try again in the spring," he told me as we drove to Chicago the weekend of the race. Always a competitor, he had set a goal of finishing in four hours or less. I just hoped he'd finish.

The marathon began on a chilly October morning. Hours passed while thousands of runners pounded 26 miles of Chicago pavement. I worried about whether Witek's body would be able to withstand the enormous strain. I knew he had trained carefully, but I couldn't forget that just six months ago he was lying near death in the ICU. As he told me after the race, he was having similar thoughts.

"During the run," he said, "I had time to think. And I realized that it was not important how fast I could do it, just that I could do it. I thought of the sickness—how I had to relearn how to walk, to run. I knew it would be unfair to be disappointed with the time. I was thankful just to be alive, to be there, to be able to run at all. I didn't want to demand too much from the world, or from myself. After I realized where I'd started from six months ago, I ended up enjoying myself during the run, talking to people, enjoying the scenery of Chicago and the whole experience of running my first marathon."

Witek crossed the finish line after running for 4 hours and 32 minutes. Yes, he was exhausted. Sure, he had screaming muscles and blistered feet. But on his weary face he had a satisfied smile.

He had wrestled the lion who'd attacked him last March, and—with the power of prayer and his own perseverance—he had won.

BY DIANA THRIFT

"I was thankful just to be alive, to be there, to be able to run at all."

IN PRAISE OF THE ORDINARY

◆ ◆ ◆

*A*T WAS FIVE DAYS before Christmas when the orthopedic surgeon walked into the examining room and said, "Your daughter has a tumor in her arm." He put the X rays up on the screen and pointed to a dark area in the bone just below her right shoulder.

My wife and I looked at one another in disbelief. Maddy, our nine-year-old, had always seemed as healthy as any other kid—until she took a spill on the playground earlier that day. Since then, her right shoulder had swelled up to the size of a grapefruit, and she'd been unable to move her right arm.

I had taken her to the emergency room that night, expecting to bring her home in a cast. But the doctor took one look at her X ray and said, "This doesn't look right."

I stared at the film on the backlit screen. Her humerus bone had little hairline fissures running all through it.

"You see," the doctor explained, pointing to the cracks radiating out across her bone, "this isn't what we expect to find in a fracture like this."

Before we left, the Urgent Care staff called an orthopedic specialist and lined up an appointment for 9:00 the next morning. Then they gave us the X rays and sent us home.

Maddy's joy and wonder are as strong as ever, and I thank God every day that I'm allowed to be a part of her world.

The next morning, the orthopedic surgeon X-rayed both of Maddy's arms. We could see a marked difference between the two: The right humerus bone sort of puffed out just below the shoulder; the left one had grown straight and true. The doctor confirmed that there was an unusual growth in Maddy's right arm; as to what it was, he was a little less certain. Only an MRI could give us more information. But because of the impending holidays, with everyone going on vacation and offices running half-staffed or less, it would be well after the New Year before we could get the MRI.

I spent that Christmas season in silent prayer. As any parent would do in a similar situation, I bargained with God for the health of my daughter. I offered my own well-being as an insurance policy against any harm coming to her. I begged God to make the tumor go away.

On January 17, they did the MRI.

I sat just outside the window of Maddy's room, watching her. She was taking in everything. From the moment she came out of the womb, she was fascinated with all that was around her. She looked around the delivery room like she owned the place. And she hasn't stopped since.

I watched Maddy sprout, and I was increasingly amazed by her intensity and enthusiasm. So was everyone around her. She was a whirlwind of activity—dragging pots and pans out of the cupboards, dancing at the first note of music, laughing, twirling, running, exploring, giggling almost uncontrollably. Her energy and joy were contagious.

Since then, I've watched puppet shows with my daughter providing the voice of every character. I've seen her whack piñatas into papier-mâché mush. I've been asked—and have given in—to throwing this little bundle of energy as high into the air as my arms would allow. I've seen my little girl adorned with smeared lipstick and stick-on earrings. But there's one thing I haven't seen. I haven't seen Maddy give up. Ever.

My wife and daughters have given me more fine times than any one man deserves. Having emerged from a troubled childhood, I cherish the regularity of common hours, the uneventful lunch, the boring evening at home. To me, the constancy, the regularity, the knowledge that I'm surrounded by people who love me unconditionally is more than enough to keep me fulfilled. And the threat of losing that—of losing Maddy—made it all the more special and important to me.

Even after the results of the MRI came back, the doctors still weren't certain. Finally, in January 1998, more than two years after the original accident, our orthopedic surgeon repaired my daughter's arm. The diagnosis was confirmed: benign bone cyst.

I wanted to dance and sing and shout for joy! I wanted to celebrate with Maddy—my most precious gift from God. Her hospital room was soon filled with presents and stuffed animals—apparently, I wasn't the only one who felt like celebrating.

These days, we sit around the TV room and apply vitamin E oil to her scars. We work on long division. We wrap birthday presents for friends and fight over stations on the car radio. We read stories, go bike-riding, and tell silly jokes. Maddy's joy and wonder are as strong as ever, and I thank God every day that I'm allowed to be a part of her world. It may not be the most exciting life, but that's okay with me.

I'm grateful for it. All of it. Every single second.

BY SCOTT MEMMER

THE GIFT OF LOVE

◇ ◇ ◇ ◇

F YOU HAVE something to do, someone to love, and something to hope for, every day becomes a celebration.

—ANNA TRIMIEW

A HOUSE FULL OF LOVE

❖ ❖ ❖

❖ ❖ ❖ ❖

"You know that sign that says, 'Love sees no color'? Well, that's who we are."

❖ ❖ ❖ ❖

IN A PUEBLO-STYLE house on a hill overlooking the Pacific Ocean, a remarkable family lives and loves and thrives together. Jack and Kay Corrodi created their unique family, one or two members at a time, through adoption and guardianships. They now have 16 children.

After her first husband died in a helicopter crash, Kay met Jack at a real estate seminar. Within a year, they were married. Kay, who had three adult children, always wanted to have a big family. Jack, who had grown up as the eldest of three sons, looked across a Thanksgiving table early in their relationship and said, "Next year, I want this table to be full of kids." Their wish was fulfilled several years later, when Kay and Jack's Thanksgiving table was indeed full of noisy, exuberant children.

"Our first wonderful surprise was Luci," Jack explains. "A woman wanted us to take her child and so we got Luci when she was one day old, just out of the hospital. She was such a beautiful child, it really set the tone for all the others."

Luci's siblings in the Corrodi clan came from storefront clinics in Mexico, Bolivian orphanages, hospital drug wards, and other troubled situations and homelands. Where they came from is not so important, though; what matters is that each child is now a Corrodi, welcomed and loved just as much as if he or she were biologically related to the enthusiastic Kay and Jack.

"All children come to us as strangers," Kay says. "Parents don't know their biological children at first. It's up to the adults to make a family."

The Corrodis cite their faith in God as a continual source of strength and guidance. Kay explains, "We pray a lot. We can draw on our faith when we need it." Jack concurs, "God is behind everything we do."

Jack and Kay ended up with nine boys and seven girls of African American, Caucasian, and Hispanic heritages. Growing up in this smorgasbord of love has made each child especially accepting of the different races of their classmates and friends.

"We've always known that we were adopted It didn't matter. What matters is who raised you. That's my mommy," son Bill says, pointing to Kay. "And he's my daddy. And these are my sisters and brothers, even if our skin isn't the same color."

Kay laughs. "I forget that my children are different colors from me," she says. "So one time, when someone came up to me, looked at my dark-skinned son and asked, 'Is he adopted?' I wondered, *How can he tell?* I love the fact that our family is made up of all different colors and backgrounds," Kay continues, "but we are *one family.*"

Bill agrees. "You know that sign that says, 'Love sees no color'? Well, that's who we are," he says proudly.

This family lives in a house full of love that sees no distinction based on color. A wooden sign hangs out front on which 18 faces are carved around the words, "Corrodi Hotel: No Vacancy."

BY ANNE BROYLES

THE PRINCESS
AND THE PATIENT

◆ ◆ ◆

◆ ◆ ◆ ◆

*Princess Diana
kept her promise
to a dying friend.*

◆ ◆ ◆ ◆

*A*T WAS DURING the mid-1980s that Adrian Ward-Jackson, an art dealer who was also a prominent figure in the worlds of opera and ballet, first learned that he was suffering from AIDS. Leading what the newspapers would later describe as a "discreetly gay lifestyle," Adrian shared luxurious homes in London and New York City with his companion, Harry Bailey. At first only a few close friends knew that he had been diagnosed as HIV-positive.

Gradually, however, Adrian came to terms with the disease and began supplementing his work as governor of the Royal Ballet, member of the Theatre Museum Committee of the V&A, and director of the Royal Opera House Trust by serving as deputy chairman of the AIDS Crisis Trust. It was through this charitable role that he first came into contact with Diana, Princess of Wales. Diana shared Adrian's passion for ballet, and during the next few years she went to all of the fund-raising galas that he organized.

In March 1991, Adrian was made a commander in the Royal Order of the British Empire by the Queen for his services to the arts. Naturally, Diana attended the celebratory lunch held at London's Tate Gallery. It was there that she met Angela Serota, a former dancer with the Royal Ballet who, with her two daughters, had been nursing Adrian over the past four years. Diana joined forces with Angela in caring for Adrian when his condition took a turn for the worse the following month.

Adrian's Central London apartment was situated in the upscale district of Mayfair, and for the next five months Diana would visit there almost daily—even bringing her young sons William and Harry for a visit. Diana did all this in spite of the lingering stigma attached to making contact with AIDS patients. Diana had tried to dispel this view back in 1987, when she was photographed shaking hands with a patient in front of press photographers. She was determined that her sons, the princes, would share her commitment to the struggles of others and be raised with a well-informed attitude about people with AIDS.

But Diana was not just a princess and a spokeswoman—she was also Adrian's friend. He was not just part of a cause that she took up as one of her royal duties. Diana was intent on keeping Adrian's spirits high, which she did by chatting with him about her daily activities and their mutual friends. She also read to him for hours on end, often while holding his hand. On the few days when she wasn't able to visit, Diana would still take the time to talk with Adrian on the phone. On Diana's 30th birthday, the princess was sporting a gold bracelet that Adrian had given her.

By August 1991, Adrian's health had declined, and he was checked into St. Mary's Hospital. Diana would be leaving London to go on a holiday cruise in the Mediterranean with her family, but Adrian vowed to her, "I'll hang on for you."

When Diana returned from Italy, she went straight from the royal jet to St. Mary's. The next day she left Kensington Palace with a large picnic basket for Angela, while Prince William followed closely behind. "If Adrian starts to die when I'm at school, will you tell me so that I can be there?" the young heir to the throne later asked his mother.

Diana worried about not being there herself. She had to perform her royal duty by joining her royal relatives for their annual vacation at Balmoral in Scotland. Diana did so with the understanding that Angela would call her if Adrian's condition became critical. And so it was that on Sunday, August 19, 1991, Angela made that dreaded call to the princess. Adrian had been administered the last rites. His end was near.

Despite the fact that the last flight to London had already departed— and not even a member of the Royal Family could charter a private plane at that hour in the Highlands—Diana headed for London. Together with her bodyguard (and reportedly without permission from the Queen) the "Queen of Hearts" embarked on the 600-mile, seven-hour journey by car. She arrived at the hospital at 4:00 A.M. and spent the next few hours holding her dying friend's hand.

Diana's vigil continued through Wednesday, August 22, when she spent eight hours at Adrian's bedside, stroking his hand and comforting the family. A palace aide inquired as to how long she planned to stay, and she responded, "How could I leave him now, when he needs me most?"

Diana was determined to do everything she could to offer support and comfort, and so, while news of her hospital visit leaked out to the

"Those last hours would have been much harder for him but for her support and kindness."

gathering reporters and press photographers, she remained resolutely at Adrian's bedside. "She proved to be a very, very special friend of Mr. Ward-Jackson," a nurse later commented. "Those last hours would have been much harder for him but for her support and kindness."

For her part, Diana was in desperate need of some rest herself, so at 10:00 on the evening of August 22, she retired to Kensington Palace. Three hours later, 41-year-old Adrian Ward-Jackson died. Angela phoned the princess, and within half an hour Diana was back at the hospital, saying a sad goodbye to her friend and kissing him lightly on the forehead. Diana and Angela joined hands and prayed the Lord's Prayer.

Diana stayed with Adrian's grieving relatives and friends until 8:00 in the morning. A few days later, she and Angela stood side by side at Adrian's funeral.

The five months that Diana spent caring for Adrian Ward-Jackson helped to give her a clearer perspective of her own life: "The people's princess" had lost a trusted friend, but in the process, she gained a sense of purpose that would ultimately provide her with strength for her own trying times.

"I reached a depth inside which I never imagined was possible," Diana wrote to Angela shortly after Adrian's memorial service. The friendship between the princess and the patient had been invaluable to all involved. Diana had vowed to stay with her friend until the end, and she had kept that promise. In so doing, a dying man gained comfort and spiritual peace, while a caring woman rediscovered her true inner strength.

BY RICHARD BUSKIN

ROSES FROM JOE

❖ ❖ ❖

*J*OE, MY VERY good friend of three decades, loved anything that was a challenge. If you said it couldn't be done, Joe would show you a way. As it turned out, he'd continue to prove me wrong, even after he'd passed away.

Joe was born during the Depression, so he was frugal with himself— but never with others. He would help people he didn't even know. He did a stint in the military for two years, and he made many great friends, including some in Sturgis, South Dakota, where he became interested in motorcycles. Joe was an avid motorcycle buff and loved racing. He traveled to Sturgis every year for the week-long motorcycle rally. He would plan all year for that vacation and always returned with many pictures and lively stories.

A smoker from boyhood to the late 1970s, Joe eventually developed asthma and emphysema. He was also a certified welder in a chemical plant until he retired at age 65, so his lungs took quite a beating. But even while he was sick, Joe maintained three properties he owned, and he cut, split, and stacked a year's supply of wood for his father-in-law.

As Joe aged, his breathing got more labored. His frail body showed signs of failing, but still he never complained. He just kept pushing on. He was a man of few words, but when he had something to say, people listened.

Every day, Joe stopped by our house to have coffee or tea and a snack. If it was breakfast time, he would have toast burnt to a crisp that was cooled and then piled with butter. At lunchtime, he'd have an olive sandwich. He would always stay about 20 or 30 minutes and then be on his way.

You could set your clock by Joe and his old cronies. They would meet at the local VFW at the same time every day to chat and goad one another. As time passed, the group kept getting smaller, and Joe was eventually the last one left. His health began to deteriorate more rapidly, and he was frequently admitted to the hospital for breathing treatments. But each time he was released, he'd be back out in his 1952 International truck, hauling wood and never slowing down, even though walking just 15 feet was very hard for him.

One summer afternoon, my wife, Judy, and I were about to head out, and Joe stopped in as we were leaving. We met him on the sidewalk under our rose trellis, which was adorned with Seven Sisters roses. They were beautiful and full, like a blanket of pink and white. Joe admired the lush array of flowers but pointed out that we should include some red ones, too. We told him we had planted some, but they didn't take.

Three months later, in September, Joe was hospitalized again, this time on a respirator. One day the call came from his wife that nothing more could be done, so they were going to take him off the machines. Judy and I rushed to the hospital to see our old friend before he passed away. We made it in time, about an hour before Joe died. Even though we weren't sure if Joe understood us, we talked to him. Before he drew his last breath, he raised up from his pillow, moved toward us, and smiled, so it seemed to us that he knew we were there. Even though we were sad about losing our dear friend, Judy and I knew that he'd had a good life and was ready to move on.

A month later, in mid-October, a heavy frost was setting in. Trees were radiant in dazzling shades of red, yellow, and brown. With autumn fast approaching, gardens were harvested, and everyone began preparing for winter.

Judy and I were walking along the sidewalk one day, discussing how Joe would have enjoyed the vibrant fall leaves. When we approached the trellis, we looked up, and both of us stared at the roses. At the very spot Joe had pointed to earlier in the year, there were two rosebuds blooming in red and white.

At that moment, we knew that Joe was with us in spirit. Wherever he was, he was still taking on new challenges and still delighting his friends.

Ever since that day, we've had a mixture of red, pink, and white roses growing where we thought the red blooms wouldn't take hold. And now every time Judy and I pass by the trellis, we think of our friend and smile when we see those beautiful roses from Joe.

BY MARTIN L. WRIGHT

Wherever he was, he was still taking on new challenges and still delighting his friends.

CUDDLED NEXT TO MY HEART

◈ ◈ ◈

"GIANT Family Size" read the cracker box in front of me.

I couldn't have said it better. Forty pounds overweight, and a whole month past my due date, I felt monstrous and miserable, like a medical freak.

Why was God allowing this to happen to me? My friends had started snickering, "You were due *when?*" Even my doctor grumped at me as if it were my own fault.

I had so looked forward to this first pregnancy. My mother, who had six children, *glowed* each time she was expecting. And *her* mother worked full-time—and still cared for 16 little ones!

My expecting friends all looked adorable in their frilly, billowy outfits. But I looked like a walrus. And waddled like one—when I could move at all. My ankles swelled so badly, I often had to keep them in buckets of ice.

And now, in the middle of this busy supermarket aisle, I suddenly developed a charley horse in both feet. I couldn't move.

I stared at the rows of cracker boxes in front of me, pretending not to notice the angry shoppers whose way I was blocking.

Then I heard a child ask, "Mommy, why does that lady look so funny?"

I shut my eyes to keep from bawling. *Oh, God, please! Can't anyone say anything nice about me for a change?*

"Dear," the mother replied, "it's because God has given her a tiny baby to cuddle next to her heart."

When I opened my eyes, she was gone. But her words have lasted a lifetime. For they were so true. And still are today.

Even after our children are born, even when they are grown up and have children of their own—no matter how big they get, or how far away they go, we mothers always "cuddle" our children right next to our hearts.

BY BONNIE COMPTON HANSON

I GAVE MYSELF AN ANGEL

◆ ◆ ◆

BOUT TEN YEARS AGO, I gave myself a birthday present: my very own angel.

I am the eldest of four children in my immediate family and the eldest of 15 cousins in my extended family. I've been taking care of babies and small children most of my life, and I've never felt a strong desire to have children of my own.

My friends, however, were all having babies—and they were all having boys. Though I enjoyed playing with them, buying things for them, and going places with them, I wanted to do the same with a girl. I wanted a girl to do things for, a girl who would need me and learn from me. Knowing there are countless children in need of compassionate mentors, I decided that would be the perfect role for me.

I didn't want to form an abstract relationship in which I just wrote a check. I wanted it to be a situation where we could develop a personal relationship. So I signed up to sponsor a Native American girl through a program that encourages personal relationships between its sponsors and students.

Native American children drop out of school at an alarmingly high rate. The program I signed up for is dedicated to keeping Native American children in school. The entire process is done through a kind of long-distance mentoring. The sponsor respects the child's culture and emphasizes the importance of education.

What started out as a simple attempt to assist a child in need turned out to be a life-changing experience.

◆ ◆ ◆ ◆

I thought I was teaching and showing my friend new things. I realized later that she was actually teaching and showing me.

I was introduced to my friend (as I now call her) through a pamphlet that included some details and a small picture. My friend is Navajo and lives in a remote area of the reservation.

I noticed immediately that we had many things in common. The eldest of several children, she was doing well in school, loved to read, and was very close to her grandmother.

We started writing, and she soon surprised me. While the organization that had put us together said most children in the program are afraid to travel, my friend asked if she could come visit me in Chicago. We checked with her mother, and I made the arrangements. Since there were no telephones on her end and they lived a long distance from a major airport, the travel planning required a major effort on her mother's part.

I treated her visit like I would any other. Before she arrived, I arranged to be free for a week and made lists of things she might like to do. But after she arrived, I realized this was no ordinary visit—an angel had entered my life.

Other children I saw at the airport had the busy look of adults. My friend, however, glowed. She was both an innocent and an old soul at the same time. She had spent the previous week in the mountains with her grandmother and great-grandmother. Neither had running water, electricity, or a telephone. They were weavers and shepherds, taking care of goats and sheep, moving between camps as the seasons changed.

When I suggested we send them postcards, she told me they only spoke Navajo and got mail when they went to the trading post once a month. "I'll see them as soon as I get back," she informed me. "There's nothing to worry about."

I noticed a feather as she unpacked. "What's this?" I inquired. "Oh," she answered, "they had a ceremony for me so I would be safe on my trip. I have to keep this while I'm here."

I live in a city with Christians, Jews, Buddhists, Moslems, and a variety of people with other religious beliefs. Different religions were not usually an issue. Here, though, was something I had not considered. I asked, the best I knew how, if she needed to do anything religious while she was visiting.

"No," came the answer. "We attend ceremonies and sings, and we believe certain things about the world, but I don't need to do anything every day or every week."

I'm fortunate to live near Lake Michigan, and the first morning of her visit my friend asked if we could go to the beach. She didn't want to swim; she wanted to see and feel. She took off her shoes and stood in the sand with the waves lapping at her feet. Gradually taking tentative steps, she ventured in until the water reached above her ankles, then she stopped and came back. She was at home in the old and new worlds, learning to live simultaneously in both.

The rest of the visit I thought I was teaching and showing my friend new things. I realized later that she was actually teaching and showing me. We went to museums, fairs, and movies. She asked typical questions, such as, "Can we go see this movie?" She asked other questions, too—ones I'd never thought about. "Does it rain this much every summer? No wonder it is so green! Were these trees always here, or were they planted by settlers?"

I shook her hands and thanked her, and she spoke a few more words in Navajo. "Remember me, my daughter," was the translation. I do and I always will.

She told me about her great-grandmother's memories of buffalo. She talked about washing clothes in a stream the week before and asked questions about an educational game she had found on my computer. When a friend came to cut our hair, she asked what happened to the hair. I said that I usually sweep it into a pile and put it in the garbage.

"My grandmother believes that you have to save and burn it. Otherwise the birds and the mice will make nests in it, and you will go crazy," she explained. "Can you give it to me?" she asked. "That way, I'll give it to my grandmother the next time I see her and she can burn it. That will make her feel better."

With mementos, packaged hair, and feather, my friend had to go home too soon. It was time for her to return to school.

After that visit, we kept in touch regularly. Often when I'd come home from a grueling business trip on the verge of being depressed, I'd receive a note from my friend, who knew just how to lift my spirits: "I just wanted to tell you how much you help me."

Then came a letter from her mother, with what felt like a bumper sticker inside. "You are more responsible for this than me. So I thought you should have it," she wrote. Puzzled, I turned the bumper sticker over. It read, "My Child is a Principal's Scholar at Chuska School."

I would often put notes in the mail (some with small gifts), so my friend knew I was thinking about her. Sometimes I asked friends and family to write, too.

The most recent time I saw my friend was when I visited where she lives. I met her family, her boyfriend, and her boyfriend's family. My friend also showed me the junior college she now attends.

Most important, I met both her grandmother and great-grandmother at their summer camp, high in the mountains. To meet both these ladies was an honor for me. I found it interesting to learn that traditional Navajo culture is matriarchal, and men marry into a woman's family.

My friend's grandmother, after moving her sheep and goats back into their pens, served us a snack. Then I sat outside with her great-grandmother underneath a shade tree.

For two people from totally different cultures, neither speaking the other's language, we had a great time! We laughed, asked questions, and bonded. My friend and her mother, translating as we talked, soon fell behind in the conversation. Then, too soon, it was time for me to go.

The matriarch of my friend's family motioned for us to wait a moment. She quickly entered her home, returning just as swiftly. She spoke something in Navajo. "She wants you to have this," said my friend's mother.

"Oh, I can't," I protested. This woman, who appeared to have nothing, was giving me a sterling silver and turquoise nugget bracelet. "If you don't take it, she will be insulted," my friend's mother said.

I shook her hands and thanked her, and she spoke a few more words in Navajo. "Remember me, my daughter," was the translation. I do and I always will.

For me, what started out as a simple attempt to assist a child in need turned out to be a life-changing experience. Although I expected to be the teacher, I ended up being a student, too. By reaching out and opening my heart, I didn't just make a wonderful new friend—I got my very own angel.

BY DEBORAH J. MILLER

THE RUSSIAN VERSION OF ME

❖ ❖ ❖

I felt goose bumps prickle my skin when I thought of God choosing me to help a woman who lived halfway around the world.

HEY SAY God works in mysterious ways and that truth is stranger than fiction. My story illustrates that both of these sayings are true.

For the past 12 years, I've been an active member of a couponer's/refund club. Through the club, people can use coupons and refunds offered by companies for purchasing their merchandise. My husband's work is seasonal, and these company offers are a great help for people, like me, who subsist on a limited income.

In 1991, a friend sent me an offer from a greeting card company. All I had to do was sign up for a foreign pen pal, stating which country I wanted my pen pal to be from. In return, I would receive a $1.50 coupon to put toward the purchase of a greeting card.

I wasn't actually that interested in the pen pal part of the deal—I just wanted that coupon! Without giving it much thought, I quickly jotted down "Russia" and mailed in the offer.

In a couple weeks, I received my coupon and the name of my Russian pen pal: Zoia Jeremko, who resided in Moscow.

I wrote Zoia a letter, telling her about myself and my family, and asking her about herself. She wrote back and told me she was 49 years old, close to my own age. She said that her husband had died of cancer, and she lived in a three-room apartment with her daughter, elderly mother, and six-year-old grandson. She worked in Moscow's largest hospital, where she was a registered nurse. She also had a degree in radiology. She explained that, in Russia, the government pays the wages of health care professionals, and Zoia was making the equivalent of $35 a month.

We corresponded sporadically for the next year. Then, after Christmas 1992, I heard no more from her. I wrote to her several times but received no response. I wrote one last letter, expressing my great concern for her, and enclosed a family picture. I finally received a reply from Zoia in May 1993; she told me she had been too depressed to write sooner.

After discovering she had breast cancer, she had undergone a mastectomy on her left breast. Russia's medical equipment, technology, available treatments, and medications are much less advanced than those in the United States. Zoia was unable to obtain even a prosthesis for her bra. Her letter outlined the terrible living conditions in Russia, which she said she could withstand, but being "so horribly maimed and mutilated," as she put it, was more than she could bear.

I felt greatly compelled to try to help her, so I took her letter to our local small-town newspaper. I was hoping one of our church groups would sponsor a trip here for her so she could obtain a prosthesis and have a mammogram done on her remaining breast. Instead, much to my surprise and great delight, the owners of a local factory donated the money for a round-trip ticket for her, and the American Cancer Association promised to give her a free prosthesis.

❖ ❖ ❖ ❖

"It is very eerie, very strange. She is the Russian version of you!" I couldn't imagine what she meant. But I found out when Zoia finally arrived.

❖ ❖ ❖ ❖

Our correspondence intensified, with letters full of excitement and anticipation. After hearing about my efforts to get Zoia to the United States, Father Korolenko, a Russian Orthodox pastor, contacted me. He and his wife regularly visit Moscow, as Mrs. Korolenko teaches English at a university there during the summer months. They were preparing for one of their trips, and they agreed to take some gifts to Zoia from me.

When the Korolenkos departed for Moscow, I anxiously awaited their return, eager to find out what Zoia was like. When they came home several weeks later, Mrs. Korolenko phoned me. I excitedly asked her about Zoia. There was a long silence and then, in an almost awestruck voice, she answered, "It is very eerie, very strange. She is the Russian version of you!" I couldn't imagine what she meant. But I found out when Zoia finally arrived on September 3, 1993.

Zoia and I both had the same sense of humor, we enjoyed many of the same things, and our thoughts and opinions were very similar. We even had the same bad left knee, which had happened because of falls we'd had! Sometimes, we knew what the other one was thinking before anything was said.

Zoia and I also shared our deep faith in God. We quickly bonded like sisters, and I grew to love her every bit as much as I would a sister. I knew she loved me in the same way.

The American Cancer Society gave her a new prosthesis, and a mammogram was taken on her remaining breast. We rejoiced and thanked God when the doctors found no evidence of cancer.

Zoia became an American citizen on March 5, 1998. Her grandson, now 11 years old, is in the United States on a student visa, and the necessary papers have been sent to immigration services to get her daughter and mother here. She has always called me her "fairy godmother," but she has helped me as much as I've helped her. She's always been there for me, through good times and bad. If I get depressed, all I have to do is talk to Zoia for five minutes, and she has me roaring with laughter. If I have a problem, she imparts her keen wisdom to me.

One day while we were talking, I asked her, "Where did you go in Moscow to sign up for a foreign pen pal?" She was strangely silent and looked at me solemnly. "I never signed up for a pen pal," she said quietly. "I did not know from where you took my name. Now I know. God sent my name to you! If not for this, I would now lay in the land. I know this!"

I felt goose bumps prickle my skin when I thought of God choosing me to help a woman who lived halfway around the world—the Russian version of myself! God brought Zoia and me together in a miracle that only he could perform, and he has greatly blessed us both by doing so.

BY SHARON WATSON

SCRAPS

◆ ◆ ◆

"BUNNY NEEDS new stuffing and a patch." It was midnight when Martha heard those words, spoken by her granddaughter as she stood on the other side of the screen door. The 18-year-old held up a dilapidated cloth animal—a sharp contrast to her black leather pants and dark makeup.

"Do you have any scraps?" she asked, her voice tinged with pleading.

Oh my, Martha said to herself as she gathered the thin young lady with neon-pink hair into her arms, *this child needs a bit of patching up, too.*

Linda had finally made the leap from the unstable edge of a perilous life to the safety of Grandma's house.

After phoning her parents to say that she was fine, was not coming home, and was not with her boyfriend, Linda allowed her grandmother to tuck her into bed on the couch.

"Tomorrow, we'll clean out the sewing room upstairs and make you a place in there," Martha promised.

The older woman had just fallen asleep when she awoke to hear Linda crying and talking in her sleep. Martha sat on the steps and tried to decipher what the child was saying; she didn't want to wake her and broach the child's torment until she was ready.

The next day, they worked hard fixing up the sewing room. Afterward, Linda took a nap, ate a small supper, and took Bunny upstairs to keep her company in bed.

"Tomorrow we'll find a patch for Bunny," Martha promised, calling after her. But that night, Linda's nightmare woke them both.

Martha found her granddaughter in the kitchen. Without her dark makeup and crimson lipstick, Linda looked young and vulnerable. She tried to peer through Linda's pink bangs and into the girl's sad eyes.

"I need my sleep, child. Tell me what's got us both awake," said Martha, sprinkling sugar on some bread for cinnamon toast.

"Big clocks are after me," said Linda, trying to laugh through the brimming tears. "I'm afraid of tomorrow. All of my tomorrows. I have too many decisions: college, marriage, work, moving, staying home...." A long pause followed. "I guess Mother probably told you about some of my yesterdays," Linda finally said in a barely audible voice.

"Some of them. Why don't you tell me about the others," Martha invited, sliding the plate of toast toward her granddaughter.

As she talked, Linda absently nibbled around the edges of a piece of toast. *Like a bunny*, Martha smiled to herself, remembering the day many years before when they'd made hot chocolate and cinnamon toast and then invited the stuffed pet to their "party." That day, Linda's problems had been easily fixed; tonight's were made of darker stuff. But none so bad, Martha thought, that they couldn't be mended.

In the morning, Linda brought the bag of quilt scraps downstairs. Martha had her sort through them at the kitchen table.

"This is the Christmas dress you made me when I was in kinder-garten!" Linda cried, pulling out a square of crimson plaid taffeta. Martha picked up a flowered fabric. "These were curtains for your tree house. And this one," she said, holding up a lavender lace, "was your junior brides-

"I've been planning a quilt of your life since before you were born," explained Martha. "I just haven't gotten around to piecing it together."

maid's dress when Aunt Laura got married. You grew two inches between the day I cut it out and the wedding. See, I had to let down the hem."

"I can't believe you kept all the scraps," mused Linda.

"I've been planning a quilt of your life since before you were born," explained Martha. "I just haven't gotten around to piecing it together."

"Can we, maybe, do it in a small quilt? To hang on my wall," said Linda hesitantly.

Which wall—college, home, or a working girl's apartment? Martha wondered to herself. "Why, that would look real nice," she said.

They worked for the next few weeks connecting pieces of this and that into a thing of beauty. All the while, they talked, laughed, and even cried a time or two. One day, Linda spent a few hours on the phone; a few days later, packages began arriving from colleges. Linda began wearing one of her grandfather's old dress shirts she'd found in the rag bag. She'd washed and ironed it and wore it tied around her waist.

Her nightmares lessened. Like the quilt coming to life under their hands, Linda seemed to be piecing together her life, bit by bit.

"How about adding this?" Linda held up a square of black leather. "I cut up my pants—to make Bunny a new collar," she said sheepishly.

Martha smoothed it with her gnarled fingers. "Let's embroider the date on it," she suggested casually, "in pink thread, perhaps?"

"To match the color of my hair?" Linda asked. She saw the smile behind her grandmother's innocent remark.

"Why, of course, child," said Martha. "It's the pink I look for in every sunrise. It's one of my favorites—the color of tomorrow."

BY MARGARET ANNE HUFFMAN

MISTER ROGERS
A Gift From God

◇ ◇ ◇

*H*OW OFTEN have you heard—or used—the nostalgic opening line, "When I was a child…"? I have a wonderful conclusion to that opener because in 1954, "when I was a child," I was blessed with the company of Mister Rogers. I never really saw him, and considering the magic surrounding him, I didn't even know that his was the voice of the puppets I saw on TV. Nevertheless, he was there, behind the scenes of a newly established "community supported" television station.

THE BIRTH OF A NEIGHBORHOOD

Pittsburgh's WQED (the nation's first public television station) hired Fred McFeely Rogers in the early 1950s to develop its program schedule. There was a growing need for children's programming, and, fortunately for me and millions of children to come, Fred Rogers decided to start fulfilling that need.

With host Josie Carey and a cast of puppets that included King Friday XIII, Daniel Striped Tiger, and Henrietta Pussycat, Fred Rogers entered the hearts and homes of any Pittsburgh household that owned the new invention known as television. His show was called *The Children's Corner,* and it was the award-winning precursor to *Mister Rogers' Neighborhood.* It didn't matter to me or Fred Rogers's other young viewers that the show was only broadcast in black and white or that the signal faded from time to time—to us, it was mesmerizing.

While Josie chatted with us on the air, puppeteer Fred Rogers dashed around behind the scenery, bringing each character to life; he also played musical instruments and did some work behind the camera. This explains why Mister Rogers always wore his trademark sneakers! As puppeteer, musician, producer, director, and camera operator, he was always dashing from place to place—and he wore sneaks to keep the noise down. Although he has changed his shoes many times, he's never changed his tradition of wearing sneakers on the set.

SPREADING GOOD NEWS TO EVERY CHILD AND FAMILY

In his time away from the WQED set, Fred studied child development and entered the Pittsburgh Theological Seminary. He was ordained as a minister by the Pittsburgh Presbytery in 1962 with the charge to "continue his work with children and families through the media." The following year, Rogers moved to Toronto, Ontario. There he began his career in front of the camera—not as *Reverend* Rogers, but as the now-familiar Mister Rogers, in a 15-minute children's series called *MISTEROGERS.* He didn't have a church, he had a neighborhood. And the good news he preached was that each one of us is special.

Fred Rogers returned to Pittsburgh in 1964, and, starting in 1966, his programs were distributed to a few other educational stations, then nationwide to other Public Broadcasting stations. The good news was now being spread across the country…and, in time, around the world.

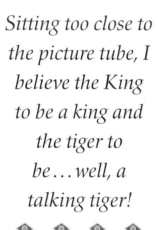

Sitting too close to the picture tube, I believe the King to be a king and the tiger to be…well, a talking tiger!

CONTINUING THE WORK THAT HE BEGAN...

Fred still writes and produces several programs a season, keeping the long-running series consistent and contemporary. And *Mister Rogers' Neighborhood* remains a favorite of children everywhere. When I see one of my nieces or nephews—and now grandnieces and grandnephews—curled up in front of a TV listening to the voice that carries me back more than four decades, I am drawn to watch. Mister Rogers buttons his cardigan and ties those sneakers, and I'm a child again. Sitting too close to the picture tube, I believe the King to be a king and the tiger to be...well, a talking tiger!

On February 25, 1999, 45 years after he began one of the most-treasured careers in the television industry, Fred McFeely Rogers was inducted into the Television Hall of Fame. For almost half a century, he has encouraged children to believe that they are special. In that time, he has been rewarded with Emmys, Peabodys, and more than 30 honorary degrees. But I think you'll agree that, because of the blessings he has brought to so many children, Fred Rogers's greatest reward awaits him in heaven. Thank you Mister Rogers, from all of us—you truly are a gift from God.

BY REBECCA LISLE

Pennies From Heaven

◈ ◈ ◈

"I JUST MISS HER so much. I'd give anything to talk with her for five minutes."

There was a long pause on my end of the line.

Pat had been my friend for many years, and although we didn't get to visit face-to-face very often, we were great phone buddies. I searched desperately for the right words to comfort her. The simple truth was that I didn't know how she felt. She had recently lost her mother to cancer, and I could only imagine the pain she was feeling. I had watched her go through the different stages of grief, offering support when I could, but the loneliness in her voice told me she needed something special…something only a mother could provide.

"Things are going to work out. I'll call you in a couple days," I said, helplessly. I wasn't sure what else to say.

Pat and her mom had been extremely close. Pat's mother was her friend, counselor, and, most important, someone who loved her unconditionally. Pat credited her with being the real strength of the family, the dependable one during life's storms. She had always been there for her only daughter to provide emotional or physical support. Since her mom's death, Pat had been struggling with some personal battles, and the advice her mom would have offered was sorely missed. Being unable to dial the phone and hear her mother's familiar, comforting voice was heart-wrenching for her.

"It's your interfering friend with her weekly call," I said when Pat answered the phone. "How's it going?"

"Don't ask unless you really want to know," she began.

"That bad, huh?"

"Yeah. I'm having some major problems with one of my supervisors at work. This week has really been rough. I can't believe I'm saying this, but I've actually thought of leaving. I just don't want to make a mistake. You know how I dislike change. It's a big step, and I've got to think of what's best for my family as well as myself."

Pat had been with the same company for years. I knew it had to be something serious for her to even consider a new job.

"Is it something you want to talk about?" I asked.

"Not yet. I've got to think this one out first."

I knew this was the final blow in a year loaded with disappointments. "Don't forget I'm here when you're ready," I said. "I'll be praying for you."

We ended our conversation with the usual promise to call. As much as I wanted to help, I felt useless. Pat's voice was so full of sadness; she seemed to be sinking lower into this painful part of her life, and I didn't have any real words of comfort. It was a downward spiral that even she seemed unable to stop.

I thought of Pat often that week, but neither of us called the other. I knew her well enough to know that her silence meant she needed some time alone. I decided that if I still hadn't heard from her by the weekend, I would call and insist that she tell me what was going on. I suspected that what she really wanted was motherly advice—the one thing no one could provide.

She told them to look at the penny whenever they missed her, and they would know she was thinking of them, sending them her love.

As often happens with good friends, while I was thinking of her, she called. When I answered the phone, I was surprised to hear a cheerful voice on the line.

"Got a minute?" Pat asked. "Sorry I haven't called, but I've really been having a hard time of it. Things at work have gone from bad to worse. I finally decided I couldn't possibly stay, but I couldn't bring myself to leave. Every day I felt more and more like I didn't belong anywhere. My head told me I wasn't being reasonable, but my heart just felt broken. I'd leave work and cry all the way home. I don't think I've been this upset since Mom passed away."

"But you sound great, like your old self. What changed?" I asked.

"It all started a couple days ago. I went over to visit Dad, and while I was there we started looking through some family things—you know, pictures and letters, stuff like that. Then Dad showed me something he had found in a box of Mom's personal things. Taped inside the cover of Mom's Bible was a penny—a bright, shiny penny. He reminded me that my niece had given it to Mom when she was sick, as a constant reminder of her love for her ailing Granny."

"That's sweet.... Why a penny?"

"It was something Mom started years ago when all the grandchildren were small. My brother's children were going away to live in another state, and she gave each of them a penny. She told them to look at it whenever they missed her, and they would know she was thinking of them, sending them her love. It got to be a family thing after that—a kind of unspoken symbol of our love for one another. Especially when we were separated from the family... Mom would faithfully include a penny each

"Mom has never stopped looking out for me.... She never will."

time she wrote. This all came back to me when Dad showed me how she kept the last penny she ever received and taped it where it could never be lost—inside her Bible."

"That's beautiful, Pat. Sounds like a great family tradition."

"That's exactly what it was. And the great thing about traditions is that they go on as long as there's a family. That night I thought a lot about how important those pennies used to be to me. But the next morning, after I got to work, all the problems there pushed those comforting thoughts from my mind. I looked around me at the people I work with and wondered if anyone really cared how miserable and out-of-place I felt. I just wanted the day to end so I could go home and hide from the world. Right before I left, Dad called and asked me to drop by the store and pick up a few things for him. I didn't really feel like doing it, but he hardly ever asks anything of me, so I agreed. In my long, silent drive, I doubted I'd ever be free from this deep sorrow. I know it doesn't make sense, but I kept thinking that Mom would have told me what to do. She's the only one who would have understood all the details and why I was so troubled. I didn't want to make any more decisions or deal with more disappointments, and I knew Mom would stand in the gap for me. Do you know what I'm trying to say?"

"I think so," I said softly.

"When I got to the store, there was a parking space up close. I pulled in, grateful that at least one thing had gone right today. I remember thinking, just as I turned off the motor, that I had never felt so alone in my life. I opened the door to step out, and something caught my eye. I looked down and there it was right beside my foot.…" Her voice trembled.

"What was there?"

"A penny—a bright, shiny penny. When I reached down to pick it up, I could hardly see for the tears in my eyes. But it was different this time. I was crying because I knew the penny was there especially for me—a way of letting me know I'm not alone, and that Mom has never stopped looking out for me.... She never will."

I knew she was right and, to my relief, I knew she was beginning to heal. As we hung up, Pat promised to call me soon with word about the new job she was applying for. She was ready to face the world again with peace in her heart and a penny in her hand. Sometimes, it seems, one penny from heaven is more valuable than all of King Solomon's gold.

BY JO UPTON

FINDERS, KEEPERS

◆ ◆ ◆

I DON'T REMEMBER my parents, and the only home I knew to speak of was a tall, red building downtown with green shutters. The only family I had was a row of other little kids lined up in the hallway waiting their turn to take a bath. Depending upon "the season of need," as Miss Ellen used to say, the number of kids varied.

Miss Ellen also used to say I was born under a cabbage leaf out by the kitchen steps so that when she opened the door to gather greens for lunch, there I was. I'd been left by elves, fairies, or the stork, depending upon which tale she told that week.

It didn't matter, because I was just visiting. I chose to think of myself as a traveler from the faraway places Miss Ellen read about to us. My parents, I insisted, had left me for a brief stopover on the way home. I needed to be ready to leave with them whenever they came back for me.

Truth be told, the only faraway places I ever visited were several foster homes. People always found my shy self too frustrating to make a long-term investment in. "She never settles in," explained one lady. "She's like a butterfly poised to fly on." But Miss Ellen had always cautioned us not to talk to strangers, and these foster parents, well-meaning as they might be, were strangers to me.

While I was visiting the foster homes, I was polite and always kept my dress, blouse, jeans, and socks folded in a tan suitcase someone had

◆ ◆ ◆ ◆

It didn't matter, because I was just visiting. I chose to think of myself as a traveler from the faraway places Miss Ellen read about to us.

◆ ◆ ◆ ◆

left at The Home many children ago. I carried the book I was writing inside my undershirt. I think that scritchy sound was one of the things foster ladies didn't care for. Especially since I wouldn't show the book to them. But, as I told Miss Ellen the last time I came back to her, I was writing *The Story of My Life* and I needed to have it close to me at all times. I showed her the family portrait I was drawing. It had a mother, a father, and usually a brother. Sometimes I changed the color of the mother's hair and how big I drew the brother and father, but the one thing I never changed was the small black dog on a leash that stood beside me. In the

portrait I wore my best dress, and my yellow hair was braided carefully into two straight ropes tied with red ribbons. The dog wore a red collar.

I was about eight years old when the Hendersons took me for a weekend. There was a mother, a father, and a chubby baby boy with no teeth. He smiled at me as I sat

beside his car seat on the way to their house. I got to sleep in a room all by myself, since they thought I'd like that. It was too quiet, though, so I made myself a nest on the floor beside the baby's crib. The next night, Mr. Henderson fixed me a cot in the baby's room. I liked hearing his little snores.

I drew "ZZZs" above the baby's head in my family portrait. I worked on it a lot that weekend and the next time I came to visit, too. The mother was getting to look a lot like Mrs. Henderson, who said I could call her Mollie. Mr. Henderson was Tom. They called the baby Jake.

Adoption, Miss Ellen said, is when a family decides to keep you. The Hendersons wanted to adopt me. I didn't tell Miss Ellen good-bye because I knew I would be back. I always was.

I was polite to the judge who asked how I liked living with the Hendersons. "Fine," I said, "but I'm just visiting." And it was fine. I slept in baby Jake's room but kept my things in what the Hendersons called my room. It was lilac and pink, my favorite colors. I colored the background of my family portrait to match. I put my crayons in the top drawer of the empty dresser but kept my suitcase under my cot in Jake's room. *The Story of My Life* was getting so thick I asked Mrs. Henderson for a paper sack to carry it in. She made me a drawstring bag. It was turquoise, another of my favorite colors.

One day, after I came inside from playing, there was a box on the floor of my room. It was tied with a pretty bow. Mrs. Henderson stood in the doorway. "Open it," she said, smiling. I carefully unwrapped it, folding the wrapping paper neatly so I could use it to make a cover for *The Story of My Life*. Inside the box was a big ball of string. That was all. A piece of string led through a hole in the bottom of the box. "Why don't you see where it takes you," invited Mrs. Henderson.

Holding the string like a fishing line, I followed it all the way to the den, where it was wrapped around lamps, chairs, and the television, out to the kitchen, back upstairs, and finally out the back door to the garage.

There, with the string tied to its red collar, was a curly black dog.

"Mine?" I asked, scarcely daring to breathe.

"To keep. Like you," my new mother said. "Forever."

BY MARGARET ANNE HUFFMAN

I didn't tell Miss Ellen good-bye because I knew I would be back. I always was.

IN PURSUIT OF THE GREAT SALAMANDER

◈ ◈ ◈

We were two adventurers in search of a common goal, and age was no longer a barrier.

◈ ◈ ◈ ◈

◈ ◈ ◈ ◈

*T*HERE ARE PROBABLY a thousand reasons why a self-respecting grandmother such as myself would dare to venture down a steep, mud-slicked hill to a creek filled with crayfish, snakes, and salamanders. Only one reason was good enough for me: the need to spend time and share interests with my adventurous 14-year-old grandson. Although I had plans that sunny afternoon three years ago, I decided to put them aside. I was drawn to accompany Jason on his pursuit of salamanders.

It was a breezy, comfortable day down at our cabin, one that lured Jason to the wonders of nature. He walked easily down the muddy hill toward the creek, where creepy crawly things found refuge under rocks and leaves.

The hunt was on, and surefooted Jason glided nimbly down the hill. I, on the other hand, made my way down slowly, clutching a makeshift cane to steady my unsure steps. I wondered silently how I could have gone from being so agile to a somewhat clumsy woman in such a seemingly short span of time.

Wasn't it just yesterday that I carried Jason in my arms and then watched him crawl and finally take his first steps? I had held his hand many times to keep him from falling, and now here he was, waiting for me on the hill with his outstretched hand, prepared to steady me. Our roles had reversed in an instant.

With my hand in his, I realized that we had crossed the line of what is commonly known as the "generation gap." We were two adventurers in search of a common goal, and age was no longer a barrier.

What happened in the next two hours can only be described as natural, without precedence or restrictions. Jason groped in the mud, digging around and removing rocks just to find a sneaky, slippery salamander. I probed with my cane and tried to uncover their secret hideouts, never getting close enough to actually touch one. Together, Jason and I became peers.

This was no everyday grandmother–grandson situation. This was an afternoon arranged by the Lord himself. Conversation was light and interrupted only by an occasional yell, announcing that another salamander had gotten away. Although I felt rather helpless and superfluous, Jason egged me on. I wallowed in mud and water, my shoes encased in a quicksand-like substance that held me in place and slowly lowered me deeper into the soft ground.

This may have seemed like an ordinary day to any onlooker, but to me it was a definite setup by the Lord. He saw the need for the young and the old to put aside all other plans and share a special time together.

As I finally tried to make my way back up the hill, the path became slicker, and it was almost impossible for me to get any traction. As I took one big step and reached for a nearby tree to steady me, my ride in the mud began. I fell to my knees and slid backward toward the creek. As I giggled uncontrollably, unable to steady myself, Jason yelled to me that he could not leave his spot because there were so many prized salamanders there. After he made sure I wasn't hurt, he laughed at my mud-caked image.

I clawed and groped my way back up, grasping at any tree or root I could find, and was finally able to stand up. There I found myself face-to-face with my grinning husband. He had been watching me slip and slide in the mud for about five minutes, and the twinkle in his eyes told me I must have put on an enjoyable show.

Even though neither of these brave men had rushed to my rescue and I was now covered in gooey mud, it really didn't matter. The most important thing about that beautiful afternoon was that I got to share Jason's world, if only for a short time. (I don't think I could have survived a much longer period.)

The Lord whispered in my ear that day, "Children's children are a crown to the aged, and parents are the pride of their children" (Proverbs 17:6). It would have been a real pity if I hadn't listened. For while Jason was searching for salamanders, I found that sharing time with him—even in the mud—was the real blessing.

BY ELEANOR M. BEHMAN

> *He had been watching me slip and slide in the mud for about five minutes, and the twinkle in his eyes told me I must have put on an enjoyable show.*

RAISING THE LIGHT OF LIBERTY

◈ ◈ ◈

*I*T WAS LOVE at first sight.

He was a small, high-risk preemie, born and abandoned on the same day. She was a neonatal intensive care nurse assigned to him in the hospital nursery. Both the infant and his nurse seemed determined that he would live.

"Thrive," Janet corrects with a smile.

And thrive he did, moving from high-risk to stable to doing just fine. It didn't matter to his nurse that he'd been born with a misshapen left arm and hand, a crooked spine, and without the genes needed to make him grow tall.

Janet reminded the baby as she rocked and fed him in the nursery, "You can be as tall as you need to make a difference where you're needed, and whole enough to help others."

A tough assignment for a throw-away baby.

"He'll need lots of help," the doctors said worriedly.

He needs a mother, Janet thought, inspired and amazed at the infant's valiant struggle.

The thought so galvanized Janet that she became a licensed foster mother, prepared a furnished at-home nursery, christened the baby David—figuring he'd already met Goliath and won—and took him home.

◈ ◈ ◈ ◈

"You can be as tall as you need to make a difference where you're needed, and whole enough to help others."

◈ ◈ ◈ ◈

His freedom had been vitally important to him long before he understood the concept of it.

"My son, my special boy," she lullabied in the hours it took to calm him after the surgery to fuse his spine, another to graft a bone in his left arm, and another to fashion a usable hand. She sang again to celebrate the finalization of her adoption of David.

As he grew, David could climb to the tallest branch in any tree, swim like an otter, and turn his mother's hair gray with his bicycle antics. He met, overcame, and surpassed any obstacle put in his way—even school, where things much less inhibitive than a misshapen hand or shortened stature slow many children down.

"Not my David," Janet thought proudly. His freedom had been vitally important to him long before he understood the concept of it.

In view of this, his teachers agreed in early September, it was no surprise that as soon as David read the story "Lady in Trouble" in his third grade *Weekly Reader*, he was first in line with a plan to help.

The Statue of Liberty needed refurbishing in time for a special Fourth of July celebration. The grand old lady's facelift, according to the story, would cost a fortune that no one was willing to pay.

David shared his idea with his mother. "Do you think I can do it?"

"Of course," Janet replied, already rummaging through a drawer for the paper, pens, and scissors she knew her son would need.

Those David didn't inspire, he nagged into helping. His handwritten posters covered telephone poles and fenceposts; his letter to the editor was printed verbatim in the local newspaper. Classmates and then the community began dropping pennies, nickels, and dimes into his home-made bucket. Each night, with Janet's help, David tallied up his efforts, never mind that he spent his evenings in a steel-and-leather back brace or that his remade arm and hand ached from making posters and carrying a bucket door to door.

When the folks in Washington heard about this pint-sized hero, they invited him to the White House.

"I'm bringing my mom, Your Honor," he printed on his RSVP.

On a cloudless fall day, Ronald Reagan, the President of the United States, honored David for his patriotic efforts. "I am honored to meet you," President Reagan said to the boy who'd raised the flame of independence high enough for all to see what a difference anyone can make.

Janet had known all along that her son was special. From the beginning, she had seen potential in a baby nobody else wanted. Although David had many physical handicaps, Janet made sure he was never limited by them. By teaching David to believe in himself and the power of his dreams, Janet had taught her son the true meaning of freedom.

BY MARGARET ANNE HUFFMAN

SWEET MR. STIREK

◆ ◆ ◆

*T*HERE ARE NO photographs, no gifts, no tangible objects to enhance the memory of my childhood friend, Mr. Stirek. Even the house where he used to live has been remodeled, so there's nothing familiar about it.

The day I first met this special man, I'd helped my brother, Bob, with his new afternoon paper route. "He'll never finish without your help," my mother insisted. So, grudgingly, I went along.

"Come on in," the elderly man with an easy smile said when I brought the newspaper to his door. It was the end of the route, and I was tired and cold, but I looked to Bob for assurance.

"Sure," he said, and whispered to me, "Leroy told me about him." (Leroy was the former paperboy.) So we stopped for a rest.

The old home was small and neatly kept, but plain. No knickknacks on tables or shelves. No photographs or paintings on the walls. Although two women also lived there, nothing feminine or flowery gave any hint.

We sat at the dining room table. Mr. Stirek introduced himself and offered us some hot chocolate. "Would you like to play cards?" he asked. We didn't know at the time, but that question was the beginning of our card-playing education. In time, Mr. Stirek taught every child in our family (eight of us) Seven-Up, Crazy Eights, Casino, Hearts, 500 Rummy, Double Solitaire, and Pinochle. As we left that first day, after a short time of card-playing, he invited us to come over any time and play.

◆ ◆ ◆ ◆

Mr. Stirek had no children, but he knew how to please children.

◆ ◆ ◆ ◆

When we took him up on his offer, his sister-in-law Jo-Jo, who drank her coffee out of old instant coffee jars and smoked lots of cigarettes, played cards with us.

Mrs. Stirek didn't play. She watched soap operas or went to visit her neighbors. Sometimes she would try to butt into an official card-playing disagreement between her sister and her husband, and was told not-so-politely that she should mind her own business.

At first, the card games interested me only slightly. I went mainly for the candy. I had a vague memory of Mom telling me not to take candy from strangers, but when Mr. Stirek led us to the kitchen on that first day and showed us a drawer full of Milk Duds and Good & Plentys, I forgot Mom's warning. Besides, Leroy had been there, and he was still okay.

The candy, which remained the same over the years, with an occasional Good & Fruity thrown in, played an important part in the ritual at Mr. Stirek's. He never got it out when we first arrived. Was he afraid we'd take the candy and leave and not play cards? He handed it out when he was ready—one box each time.

Going to Mr. Stirek's became a pleasant habit, and I went there at least once a week—even offering to help Bob with his route so we could stop by together. We went more often in the summer. I stayed for up to two hours each time.

Mr. Stirek had no children, but he knew how to please children. He had the playful disposition of a child, yet seemed a hundred times wiser. I don't remember him ever complaining about anything, and along the road of his 70-some years he seemed to have picked up no bitterness. As time went on, I grew to love playing cards, because he did. He would have made an excellent teacher. He had miles of patience, and he could make learning even difficult card games great fun.

I remember once I ran away from home and went to Mr. Stirek's house at night. We never went there after dark, so he must have guessed something was wrong. He didn't interrogate me or panic as some people might have. We just played cards. He gave me room to think and come back to my senses. Within an hour, I headed for home. My parents grounded me for not coming home on time. (I never admitted I had run away.) It was okay, though; it felt good to know I had a place to go, a safe haven with someone who never said a critical word and who offered total acceptance.

I wonder how I could have spent so much time with someone and yet know so little about him. I know he liked Arthur Godfrey, because he listened to him on the radio sometimes while we played cards. He liked to watch bowling on television and an occasional baseball game.

This gentle man rarely talked about himself or his past, but he did go on about a certain gopher who lived in his yard. He told me the gopher talked back to him whenever he was scolded for messing around in the garden. It took me a while to realize that this gopher wasn't as verbose as Mr. Stirek insisted. My friend had become so special, I easily imagined him with Dr. Doolittle tendencies.

"Does he really talk?" I asked repeatedly.

"He sure does." He smiled, and his eyes twinkled.

"Mr. Gopher, come out please," I called as I sat poised by the gopher hole on several occasions, while Mr. Stirek busied himself in the vegetable garden. Finally, one day when I stood up and started to walk away, the gopher poked his head out. But he didn't say a word. I decided he must not talk to strangers.

Mr. Stirek was such a contrast to my own grandfathers. One died when he was in his 50s. The other was not fluent in English, and he had been sick for years. Mr. Stirek was never sick. I wondered about his secret for good health. He didn't smoke or drink, and he walked places since he didn't have a car. Also, I marveled (out loud) that someone "so old" could have their own teeth—this after I asked him to "stick his teeth out" like my grandpa used to do. "Be true to your teeth, and they won't be false to you," he advised me.

Jo-Jo died first. It seemed quiet and peaceful when we played cards. Next Mrs. Stirek died. Mr. Stirek didn't seem sad, just quieter after that.

I don't remember when I stopped going to Mr. Stirek's. My adolescent mind must have convinced me there were more important things to do than hang around, playing cards with an old man. Besides, the place got crowded with my younger brothers and sisters and their friends, who also enjoyed visiting there.

Before I got around to going back, Mr. Stirek remarried (at the age of 81) and moved out of state, according to my brother. He had started walking to the local church after his wife died, and he met his new wife there. I was glad to hear "he even started reading the Bible," although it seemed like he already knew a lot about what it said by the way he lived. Frank Stirek died when he was 84.

Now, when I think back on the hours I spent at that special place, I can see the sacrifices Mr. Stirek made for us, and I understand now why

He remains my perfect model of old age—smiling, enjoying life, and passing wisdom and hope on to a new generation.

If time spent with someone is a measure of love, then he must have known how much I cared.

he didn't pass out those longed-for boxes of candy right away. Too young and self-centered to take note of it then, I now realize the Stireks barely scraped by. He must have been a retired factory worker, because he wore a blue work shirt most of the time. He didn't have a telephone or a car. His vegetable garden and fruit trees were necessities rather than hobbies. His refrigerator remained sparsely stocked, and we kids would ask "why?" between ourselves. He offered water to drink, with an occasional hot tea or hot chocolate made with tap water, or a rare iced tea. None of the adults ever ate the candy.

Some days I'm filled with regret that I never hugged him, never said, "I love you" or "I care about you." I never gave him a present or a card—I don't even know when his birthday was. But if time spent with someone is a measure of love, then he must have known how much I cared. When I could have bought my own candy and played cards with friends, I chose to be with him. He remains my perfect model of old age—smiling, enjoying life, and passing wisdom and hope on to a new generation. The card games were his vehicle for this.

I rarely play cards anymore—mostly when my brothers visit. On occasion, one of us will say, "Do you remember Mr. Stirek?" It really means, "Let's remember Mr. Stirek." So our game becomes a memorial to him—this sweet, extraordinary, generous man whom none of us will ever forget.

BY ELAINE CREASMAN